Hook, Line, & Seeker

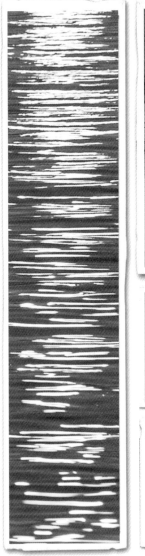

Crinkle Cove
BAIT & TACKLE

Hook, Line, & Seeker

A Beginner's Guide to
Fishing, Boating, and Watching
Water Wildlife

JIM ARNOSKY

WITH PHOTOGRAPHS AND ILLUSTRATIONS BY THE AUTHOR

SCHOLASTIC 💡 NONFICTION

A NOTE FROM THE AUTHOR

This book is intended to introduce young people to the fundamentals of fishing, boating, and watching water wildlife. The mastering of any of the outdoor skills described requires practice and hands-on supervision.

I encourage all outdoor-loving parents, teachers, and camp counselors to take your kids fishing and boating. Carry my book along to help you better understand, experience, and enjoy your time on the water together.

—J. A.

Copyright © 2005 by Jim Arnosky
All rights reserved. Published by Scholastic Inc. SCHOLASTIC, SCHOLASTIC NONFICTION, and associated logos are trademarks and/or registered trademarks of Scholastic Inc. All other trademarks used in this book are owned by their respective trademark owners. No part of this publication may be reproduced, stored in a retrieval system, or transmitted in any form or by any means, electronic, mechanical, photocopying, recording, or otherwise, without written permission of the publisher. For information regarding permission, write to Scholastic Inc., Attention: Permissions Department, 557 Broadway, New York, NY 10012.

Library of Congress Cataloging-in-Publication Data
Arnosky, Jim.
Hook, line, & seeker: a beginner's guide to fishing, boating, and watching water wildlife / Jim Arnosky; with photographs and illustrations by the author. Includes index.

1. Fishing—Juvenile literature. 2. Boats and boating—Juvenile literature.
3. Aquatic animals—Juvenile literature. I. Title.
0-439-45584-7   SN445.A762 2005   799.1— dc22
10 9 8 7 6 5 4 3 2   05 06 07 08 09
Printed in Singapore   46
First printing, May 2005

ABOUT THE ART

The color paintings in this book were done with acrylics using the dry-brush technique. (Very little water is mixed with the paint to keep the color as vivid as possible.)

The looser of the pen-and-ink drawings were taken directly from Mr. Arnosky's fishing journals. Many of them were drawn on the spot from life. All of the photos but one 35-mm photo were taken with a digital camera.

All photographs © Jim Arnosky

This book is dedicated to

Frank Schroyer.

CONTENTS

My work desk in the Florida Keys

INTRODUCTION

*W*hen I was a boy, I dreamed of adventure. I found it in three great lifelong pursuits of fishing, boating, and watching wildlife. The title of this book—HOOK for fishing, LINE for the various lines and knots used in boating, and SEEKER for finding and watching wild animals in their natural habitats—combines all three.

When you get to live out your dreams, you are required to share the experience. This is my sharing.

JIM ARNOSKY
Matecumbe Key, Florida

I CAUGHT AND RELEASED THIS BEAUTIFUL BROOK TROUT IN THE BEAVER POND BEHIND MY HOUSE.

PART I
FISHING

Then he felt the gentle touch on the line and he was happy.
ERNEST HEMINGWAY, *THE OLD MAN AND THE SEA*

I discovered fishing on my own as a boy growing up in Pennsylvania. There were scores of sunfish in a small pond near my home and they swam eagerly to a baited hook. I caught them on a simple hand-line. I've been a fisherman ever since.

I am not a person who can just sit and stare at a lovely scene. I must be in it. I have to participate. And nothing puts me in touch with nature better than casting a line into sparkling water and hooking up with a strong fish. If, like me, you cannot see a stream without feeling the urge to wade in and see what lives there; if you cannot think of anything more thrilling than having a frighteningly large and powerful fish tugging on your line; if you want to learn to bait a hook properly, land or net your own fish, and hold it yourself as you unhook it for releasing or to carry home on your stringer, then this chapter is just for you, because I'm going to share my world of fishing, from cold mountain brooks to warm tropic seas. You couldn't have a better guide.

I've been everywhere you want to go. I know the fish that live in fresh water and salt water. And I have fished for them with bait, lure, and fly.

CHOOSING AND USING FISHING TACKLE

My fishing tackle includes a bait-casting outfit, spinning gear, and a fly rod and reel. Which tackle I use depends on where I'm fishing and the fish I hope to catch.

Aside from the primitive method of using a hand-line, there are three rod and reel methods of presenting bait, lures, or flies to a fish: bait-casting, spin fishing, and fly fishing.

BAIT-CASTING outfits are used most often when fishing live minnows, trolling big spoons, or casting large surface plugs. Bait-casting rods are short and stout, and the bait-casting reels are designed to cast short distances or to simply lower a heavily weighted line down into the water from a pier, bridge, or boat.

The greatest advantage of bait-casting is working a bait to entice fish to bite. One crank

BAIT-CASTING ROD AND REEL

12

on the handle of a bait-casting reel can actually move the bait in the water. Every subsequent turn of the handle moves the bait more. A fish following a slowly moving bait will eventually succumb to the urge and seize it. Nothing can entice, hook, and haul up a large bottom-feeding fish as well as sturdy bait-casting tackle can.

SPIN FISHING is the most popular method of fishing. Spin fishing outfits let you cast farther out using lighter lines and lures. During a cast, line rapidly loops off the open-faced spool, and the lure or baited hook is literally thrown across the water. At the completion of the cast, when the lure hits the water, one turn of the reel handle locks the spool and line in place and you are ready to retrieve. It's that simple! Spinning rods—which are longer and lighter than bait-casting rods—have the flexibility to whip out a lure, throwing it far over the water.

Spinning tackle is used to fish with everything from live bait to artificial lures. With a light spinning outfit you can even cast a fly by attaching a clear floating bobber (for casting weight) a few feet from the weightless fishing fly.

SPIN FISHING ROD AND REEL

FLY FISHING is one of the oldest methods of fishing. It remains the preferred method for those who fish for the wariest fish, because it uses a hook disguised as an insect, minnow, crab, or other natural fish food, with no sinkers or bobbers to frighten the fish away.

In fly fishing, it is the line and not the lure that is weighted. Fly line is thick and heavy, and once you get ten feet of it out in the air in what is known as false casting, that ten feet of heavy fly line can pull twenty or thirty more feet of line out over the water when you finally let it go in a final true cast.

How does such a heavy line attract and catch fish? The end of the fly line is attached to an eight-to-ten-foot-long monofilament leader,

tapered to be nearly invisible at its terminal tip where the fly is attached. All of this—the heavy fly line, tapered leader, and tiny, weightless insect impostor—is catapulted out over the water by the powerful flexing of the long fly rod. In a perfect cast, the fly line lands first, the leader rolls over and lies flat and straight, and the fly does not land but gently alights on the water surface.

A fly reel is essentially used to store line. There are fly reels with wonderful and powerful drag systems built in them. But drag is used only for fighting a hooked fish. When casting a fly, the reel does very little but hold line. You do not cast off a fly reel as you do in bait-casting or spin fishing. In fly casting, you strip short lengths of fly line from the reel during each false cast until you are holding enough line to make the distance you wish to cast. Then you let it all go in the final cast. Fly casting takes practice. And practice combined with patience develops skill.

FLY LINE TO LEADER KNOT

BLOOD KNOT FOR ADDING LENGTH TO LEADER

THE PHOTO AT LEFT SHOWS ME LETTING MY FLY LINE GO IN A FINAL CAST.

FRESHWATER FISH AND FISHING

It was early May and still a bit cold in the North Country of Vermont. On Lake Champlain, where I do much of my fishing, all the boat docks were still in winter storage, piled in sections onshore. The water was too high from snow melting to install the seasonal docks and floating platforms that in just a few weeks would be busy with boaters and swimmers. I pulled a flannel shirt on, donned my warmest fishing hat, loaded my spinning tackle, and shoved off in the *Leeky Teeky*, my little inflatable boat. Its three-horsepower motor started with one strong pull of the cord. The tiny engine pushed the boat smoothly over rippling waves into a westerly wind and carried me out to the deeper water of the bay. Soon I was fishing at one of my favorite spots. It always feels good in early spring to be casting and retrieving a lure again, anticipating the sudden strike of a fish. I let the boat drift toward a rocky point of land where some weeds were sticking up out of the water and I cast a bright and shiny silver spinner lure to the edge of a large bed of submerged weeds. Bam! A bass took the lure instantly. I kept the line tight, reeling whenever I could and letting the fish run when it pulled too hard for me to reel. After a short tugging match, the fish was in my net—a nice, two-pound largemouth bass. With the bass still in the net, I carefully unhooked it. Then, grasping the bass firmly by the lower lip, I lifted it out of the net and held it high to briefly admire its colors in the soft sunlight before letting it go.

After that first fish of the season, my eyes were glued to the water, examining every ripple and wave for signs of more fish feeding close to the surface. I saw a swirl on the surface of the water amid a clump of cattails and cast the same silver spinner to the spot. Suddenly, a large

fish—an eight-pounder, at least—shot up out of the water over my lure and quickly splashed back down. I didn't hook the fish, but I got a good look at its long, streamlined shape and knew it was a salmon. Lake Champlain has a population of landlocked salmon that usually stay in the deepest, coldest water. But in spring, after the ice melts, a few salmon wander into the bays to feed in the weedy shallows. I cast my lure again to the same spot, and as soon as the lure hit the water, a big, yellow-bellied pike attacked it, snapping its jaws and cutting my line with its razor-sharp teeth before splashing away. It was a terrific thing to see and quite a surprise. I had to sit and take a moment to compose myself while tying on another lure. This time I added a wire leader to protect the line from sharp teeth.

The big pike was one of those that come to our bay each spring to spawn. The salmon must have been lurking around the pike's spawning bed. And when I cast the second time, the pike, already on the defensive, lashed out viciously at my flashing silver lure.

After my encounter with the pike, I caught

three more hefty bass—all smallmouth bass. I
lost a few more smaller pike and one very heavy
fish that I believe was a large, sluggish bowfin.
There were also plenty of sunfish chasing but
never biting any lure. I fished until the sun began
to set and the air turned from cool to cold. It felt
as if time had slipped backward into winter. I
gathered my collar around my neck and pulled
my hat down around my ears to stay warm. Just
as the sun was disappearing and I was about to
call it quits, I made one last cast. Another smallmouth bass—all bronze in color, like the setting
sun's reflection on the water, attacked my lure,
thrashing and splashing on the surface all the
way to the net. It was a big, heavy fish—a
four-pounder! When I held it high, backlit
against the glow of sunset, I felt as though
I were posing for a magazine cover. All I
had read and dreamed about fishing
through the long, fishless winter had
finally, magnificently, materialized. I
lowered the gleaming fish down over
the side of the boat and released it
into the dark water. It was
getting late and colder by the

minute with the sun completely down. I started
the little engine and headed back to shore.

FISHING IN LAKES AND PONDS

A big, freshwater lake can be home to a variety
of fish. Catfish, carp, eels, bowfin, gar, bluegills,
pumpkinseeds, crappies, yellow perch, pickerel,
pike, smallmouth bass, and largemouth bass may
all be swimming in the same water, feeding in the
same places. If the lake is deep and cold enough
in spots, there may also be drum, muskellunge,
walleye, lake trout, rainbow trout, and landlocked
salmon (salmon that do not migrate to and from
the sea). Even in very small ponds that have less
than an acre of surface area, you can catch
bluegills, pumpkinseeds, and largemouth bass.
No matter what size the body of water, the habits
of fish are the same. If you pay attention to the
feeding habits of the fish in your home waters and
adjust your fishing methods accordingly, you will
be able to catch those species of fish in any water,
anywhere you go.

Freshwater Fish

PARTS OF A TYPICAL FISH

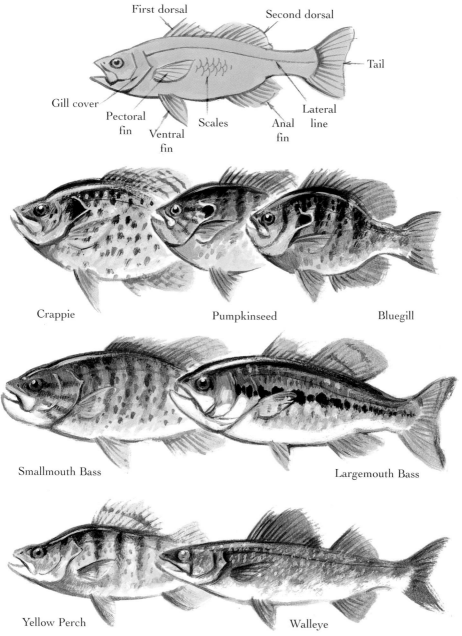

First dorsal

Second dorsal

Tail

Gill cover

Pectoral fin

Ventral fin

Scales

Anal fin

Lateral line

Crappie

Pumpkinseed

Bluegill

Smallmouth Bass

Largemouth Bass

Yellow Perch

Walleye

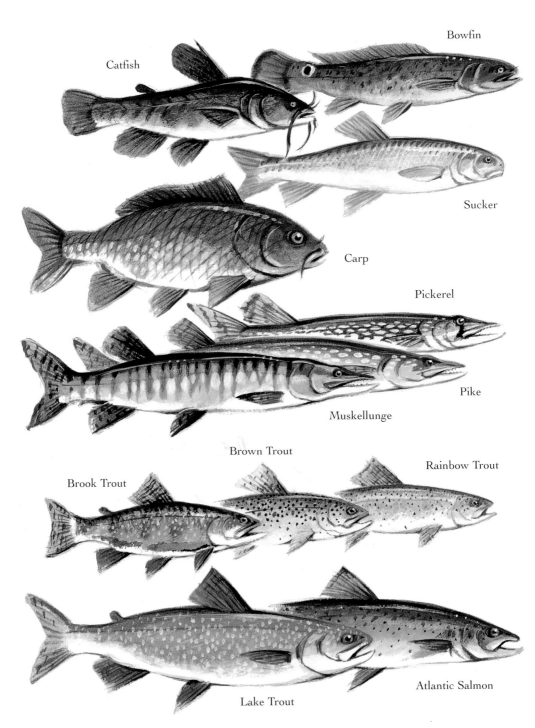

Bowfin

Catfish

Sucker

Carp

Pickerel

Pike

Muskellunge

Brown Trout

Rainbow Trout

Brook Trout

Atlantic Salmon

Lake Trout

FISHING DOWN DEEP

In lakes or ponds no deeper than twenty feet, the bottom can be as weedy and rich in food as the pond's shallow edges. Catfish and carp scour the bottom for snails, crayfish, minnows, and edible aquatic plants. Both catfish and carp find food by smell, and the most popular method of fishing for them is with smelly dough-balls. You can buy commercially prepared dough bait or you can make your own.

> *Mix 1 cup of flour with 1 cup of cornmeal.*
> *Add 3 tablespoons of water and*
> *1 tablespoon of cod-liver oil for a fishy smell.*
> *Then knead it all together into a*
> *soft, sticky dough.*

Press a wad of this stinky stuff around a sharp hook. Add a few split-shot sinkers about ten inches above the hook for weight, cast it out, and let it sink to the bottom. If there are catfish or carp in the water, they'll smell it and come to supper.

TWO SIMPLE BOTTOM-FISHING RIGS. ONE WITH SPLIT-SHOT SINKERS THAT LETS THE BAIT DRAG ON THE BOTTOM. AND ONE WITH A LARGE END SINKER THAT DRAGS ON THE BOTTOM WHILE HOLDING THE BAIT UP OFF THE BOTTOM.

The bottom of a lake or pond isn't only a place for bottom-feeders. During the hottest time of the day, pike and bass hang out in deep water, hugging the bottom, finding dark places in weeds or near boulders to stay cool. Bass and pike are primarily sight-feeders triggered into striking by the motion of swimming prey. The best way to catch them is with artificial lures that flutter, spin, wobble, dart, hop, dive, or wiggle when you pull them through the water. However, when bass or pike are hunkered down in cool, deep

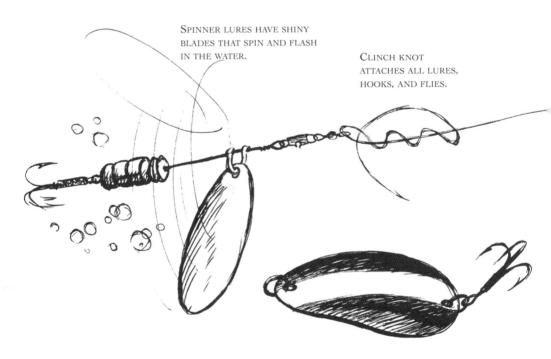

SPINNER LURES HAVE SHINY BLADES THAT SPIN AND FLASH IN THE WATER.

CLINCH KNOT ATTACHES ALL LURES, HOOKS, AND FLIES.

SPOON LURES WOBBLE WHEN RETRIEVED.

water, they tend to get lazy and won't move very far from their resting spots. At these times, you have to put your lure right in front of them to get a strike. One very effective type of lure for this kind of coaxing is the jig. Jigs are weighted hooks with soft plastic bodies or feathered skirts added for action. Fishing a jig is easy. All you do is cast, let it sink to the bottom, then hop it along with periodic jerks of your rod. You can fish a jig from shore or from a pier, bridge, or boat.

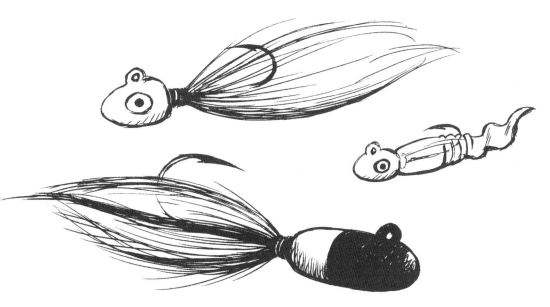

JIGS COME IN ALL WEIGHTS AND SIZES.
SOME HAVE FEATHERED OR DEERHAIR SKIRTS.
OTHERS HAVE PLASTIC TAILS.

My favorite jigging lure is called a tube
lure. A tube lure looks a little like a rubber
bullet with legs. The lure's weighted hook
has a nice wide gap for easy hooking and
unhooking. And the soft plastic tube body that
fits over the jig hook has spidery legs that wiggle
and wave enticingly in the water. On my big
boat, *Crayfish*, I like to drift over deep water
while dragging a tube lure on the rocky or weedy
bottom. The rod tip vibrates as the lure bounces
and hops down below. And when a fish hits, the
rod bends over double. I've caught some huge
bass and pike this way—ten, twenty, and even
thirty feet down. When you reel a fish caught
down deep, it feels twice as heavy as reeling it
in shallow water. A two-pounder feels like a
four-pounder, and so on. Remember to
reel whenever you can and let the fish
run when it pulls more strongly. This way
you won't break your line. I use a belt with a
rod-butt holder when fishing deep, so I have

TUBE LURE

BELT WITH ROD-BUTT
HOLDER

something to rest the rod-butt against rather than have it dig into my belly when a heavy fish is on.

If your family owns a boat, you can fish deep water by trolling or dragging a lure behind as you row or slowly motor along. As many rods as there are fishers in the boat can be trolled at once. When trolling, you want to keep the lure off the bottom so it can swim freely. Fish hugging the bottom will rise to a lure trolled just above them. And fish suspended at mid-depths in the water will follow and attack a lure trolled at their level. Lures that wobble rhythmically or swim steadily when pulled through the water are ideal for this kind of fishing. I use a wobbling spoon or a deep diving, balsa-wood minnow.

Fishermen on big lakes or bays troll using a
downrigger. A downrigger is simply a large spool
of heavy gauge wire with a big ball weight
clipped to the end. A fishing rod is placed in a
rod holder. Its line is clipped to the downrigger's
wire line and then lowered to a desired depth. If
fish are feeding at a depth of twenty-five feet, the
downrigger will keep the lure
swimming at that depth.
Once a fish hits, the fishing
line snaps free from the

A DOWNRIGGER CLAMPS
TO THE STERN OF THE
BOAT, WHERE ITS WIRE
LINE CAN BE LOWERED
INTO THE WATER.

THE FISHERMAN ADJUSTS THE
DEPTH OF THE DOWNRIGGER
WEIGHT TO GET HIS LURE
DOWN WHERE THE FISH ARE.

A TWO-TO-THREE-POUND
WEIGHT KEEPS THE LINE
TRACKING AT THE DESIRED
DEPTH.

DOWNRIGGER WEIGHT   FISHING LINE CLIP   TROLLING LURE

wire line and you bring in your catch using only your rod and reel. The fish most often caught using downriggers are the deepwater species: lake trout, salmon, and walleye. All of these fish feed primarily on schools of bait fish. A lure trolled at the proper depth looks just like a small fish that is lost and alone and easy prey.

LIPPED MINNOW

You don't have to troll at all to catch fish in mid- to upper depths. All you need is a lure that can get down to where the fish are swimming. An artificial minnow with a long plastic "lip" to make it dive will work at various depths depending on the speed the lure is retrieved. Reel it in slowly and the lip will plunge the lure a few feet down. Reel quickly and the lip will vibrate more strongly, forcing the lure to swim six to eight feet deeper.

Any metal or weighted lure will sink until you begin to reel it in. Spoons, spinners, and buzz baits all catch fish at the depth you allow them to sink before beginning to retrieve them. Drop your lure in clear water and count the seconds as it sinks to the bottom. This will show you how long it takes for the lure to sink two, four, or five feet and deeper. If the lure sinks five feet in five

BUZZ BAIT

seconds, you can cast, begin counting as soon as the lure hits the water, and begin reeling at the count of five. You will know your lure is swimming five feet underwater. If you don't catch a fish at that depth after ten casts or so, try counting to eight and fish the lure deeper. Remember: The deeper a lure is, the harder and faster it will spin or wobble. Such frantic action can twirl the lure and twist your line into knots. To prevent line twist, tie on a swivel and clip your lure to it.

No matter how fast you can retrieve a lure, the fish can swim faster.

Sometimes the faster you retrieve, the more a fish responds. Other times, only a slow retrieve will catch fish. Everything from sunfish to giant muskies are caught this way. The largest pike I've ever caught took a small silver spinner retrieved rapidly in five feet of water. That fish was thirty-eight inches long and weighed sixteen pounds. I released it.

How to Release Fish

HOLD THE FISH GENTLY AND
LOWER THE FISH TO THE WATER.

HOLD THE FISH NEAR THE WATER
AND OPEN YOUR HAND.

LOWER THE FISH INTO THE
WATER AND LET IT WORK
ITS GILLS TO BREATHE.

ONCE THE FISH REVIVES ITSELF, IT SHOULD
SWIM AWAY. IF THE FISH CANNOT REVIVE ITSELF,
GENTLY SWOOSH IT FORWARD AND BACKWARD
IN THE WATER TO GET WATER MOVING THROUGH
THE FISH'S GILLS. KEEP THIS MOVEMENT GOING
UNTIL THE FISH SWIMS AWAY.

LARGER FISH THAT CANNOT BE HELD BY
CUPPING YOUR HAND UNDER THEM CAN BE
SAFELY RELEASED BY GRASPING THEM FIRMLY
AND LOWERING THEM INTO THE WATER. FISH
WITH NO SHARP TEETH CAN BE GRASPED BY
THE BOTTOM LIP. THIS IMMOBILIZES FISH
AND MAKES RELEASING EASY.

FISH WITH SHARP TEETH CAN
BE GRASPED BEHIND THE
GILLS AND LOWERED BACK
INTO THE WATER. IF THE
FISH IS LONG-BODIED, USE
TWO HANDS TO HOLD IT—
ONE HAND BEHIND THE GILLS
AND ONE CUPPED UNDER THE
FISH'S MIDSECTION. TO
REVIVE AN EXHAUSTED
LARGE FISH, HOLD IT IN THE
WATER BY ITS TAIL AND PUSH
BACKWARD AND FORWARD
UNTIL THE FISH SWIMS AWAY.

FISHING ON TOP

Fish will rise to the surface to feed on floating insects, fleeing minnows, and swimming frogs, snakes, or mice. To get in on the surface action you have to use floating lures that imitate the shapes and movements of these surface foods. There are many different lures that are designed to entice surface-feeding fish. In my tackle box I carry a handful of old reliables.

One is a simple cigar-shaped plug known as a spook. It has treble hooks front and back. In the water the aft hardware pulls the tail of the lure down, making the spook float at an angle. When you jerk your rod, the lure lunges forward and veers to the left or right. Subsequent jerks cause the lure to lunge side to side, left, right, left, right, creating a zigzag pattern on the water. Fishermen call this "walking the dog." Fish find the motion irresistible and will shoot upward as much as ten feet to smash the zigzagging lure. The best time to fish a spook is sundown when the water becomes calm and the zigzagging motion can be detected by fish from all directions.

SPOOK AND ITS ZIGZAGGING ACTION ON THE WATER

POPPER

Another lure I always carry is a popper. A popper is a lure with a wide, concave mouth to trap air and water, making a loud popping sound each time you jerk your rod. Poppers attract fish from a distance. If I see that fish are feeding on the surface, I use a popper to get a fish's attention. Cast a popper out as far as you can and let it float a few seconds. Then twitch the rod tip to yank the lure forward an inch or two. You'll see the tiny splash and hear the pop. So will hungry fish.

My favorite lure is another surface lure known as a jitterbug. A jitterbug is a small-bodied lure with a wide metal lip that makes the lure actually crawl on water when you reel it in. The crawling action along with the soft gurgling sounds the lure makes as it moves has proven to be an irresistible combination for big fish. Bass or pike will stalk the crawling lure for five or six feet before rushing to grab it. The strikes are always vicious and explosive. In fact, it is the sudden violent strike that takes practice to be ready for and react to. I always count five seconds and then start reeling. Working the lure takes very little skill. All you do is reel it in.

JITTERBUG

OLD WOODEN LURES HAVE BECOME VERY COLLECTIBLE.
HERE ARE SOME OF THE ANTIQUE LURES IN MY COLLECTION.

I taught my two oldest grandsons — Derek, who was four, and Darren, who was eight — how to fish a jitterbug. Together we three cast our jitterbugs out onto the lake. Then, following my lead, the boys reeled slowly, stopping every few feet to let the lure float very still. Then we reeled slowly again. As we were reeling, a bass grabbed my bug. Another bass attacked Derek's. And Darren hooked a pike. We were yelping and laughing and reeling together. It was the first time the boys had fished using top-water lures. I know it won't be the last time they do so.

Sometimes it's fun to fish a soft-bodied lure on the surface. It's like working a puppet. Rubbery frogs and plastic worms float and can be worked to swim very naturally in the water. During the midday heat, big fish take refuge from the sun by finding shade under floating lily pads. A rubber worm pulled over lily pads can provoke tremendous

PLASTIC WORM WITH HOOK EMBEDDED TO MAKE THE LURE WEEDLESS

strikes from big fish cooling off below. I've had four-pound bass gobble down my lure and a mouthful of lily pads and stems. The next time you see a quiet cove covered in lily pads, think of the monster-sized fish that can be lurking underneath.

Fish feeding on top create splashes, swirls, or dimples on the water surface. You have to learn to recognize these riseforms and cast to them. When you cast to a riseform, your chances of catching a fish increase greatly. One spectacular sign of surface-feeding fish is not a riseform but a miniature event known as a bait shower. When many small fish suddenly leap out of the water in unison, showering back down together, they are fleeing a predator. Cast a balsa minnow to the vicinity of a bait shower and you may quickly discover what predatory fish caused the commotion.

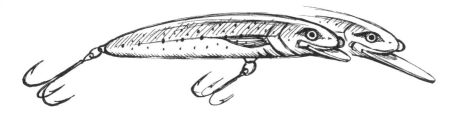

Balsa minnows float when they are still, and quickly dive when you begin to reel them in. When you stop reeling, they rise back to the surface and float until they are reeled in again. Do this over and over and you create the appearance of a wounded minnow sinking slowly, then struggling to swim again. Big fish never pass up an easy meal. That's how they get so big.

That's also how they get caught.

There will be times when fish are feeding on things so small, it just looks like they are sipping air at the surface. What they are actually doing is eating insects—aquatic or terrestrial—that for one reason or another are floating on the water. The only lure that can duplicate the look and lightness of an insect on the water is a light-wire hook dressed with buoyant deerhair or feathers.

Lures made this way are called fishing flies or bugs.

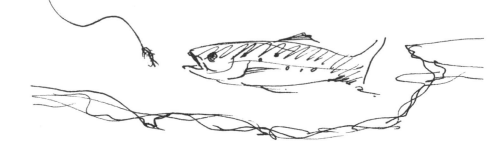

For lakes and ponds, I use one fly almost exclusively: the muddler minnow. Tied in various sizes, muddlers can imitate dragonflies, mayflies, dobsonflies, stoneflies, crickets, and grasshoppers. A muddler cast to a spot where fish have been rising is sure to trigger a strike. The fly floats like an insect until it becomes waterlogged and sinks. Then you retrieve it in short darts to make it look like a minnow swimming a few inches under the surface. Don't make the mistake of thinking that only a little bitty fish would hit such an itty-bitty lure. By using muddlers I've caught bass weighing more than six pounds. Small minnows and aquatic insects are such rich sources of protein, even the biggest fish include them in their diet.

We've fished down deep, in the middle, and on top. You'd think we'd be all fished out by now, but we've really only begun. There is much more to freshwater fishing: There is trout fishing in streams.

MUDDLER MINNOWS ARE TIED IN VARIOUS SIZES TO IMITATE MINNOWS, GRASSHOPPERS, AND AQUATIC INSECTS.

FISHING IN STREAMS

Fishing in its purest form is a communion with nature—a desire to get closer to the water, woods, and wildlife. Bird-watching and animal tracking become integral parts of an outing. And the fish you catch punctuate the story of your day. Time spent fishing is simply feeling at home in nature. And no other type of fishing puts you in the world of water and fish better than trout fishing in small streams. You hop from boulder to boulder, following the water's flow. You wade ankle deep in the current, stepping on gravel or rounded rocks. The sound of water tumbling and splashing echoes in the forest. The smell of leaves, moss, and earth saturate the air. And sunlight filtering down through the trees softly illuminates every riffle and pool.

I fish small streams using my smallest

tackle—either a tiny, four-foot-long spinning rod with no stronger than a four-pound test line, or a six-foot fly rod with a four-weight fly line. When you fish a brook walking downstream and then fish it back upstream to where you started, you do a lot of walking and some crawling to get from pool to pool. Light tackle is less to carry all day long, and the shorter the fishing rod, the easier it is for you to move through the tangle of tree limbs, brush, and vines that surround and overhang the water.

In mountain brooks and woodland streams, the trout are apt to be small. For fly fishing in small streams, any floating or sinking fly will catch trout as long as the hook is small. When spin fishing in brooks, tiny gold spinners work best. And whether you are using spin or fly tackle, you can always try bait by adding a worm to your hook.

In streams less than twelve feet wide, very little casting is necessary. Simply reach out with your rod and drop your line midstream. Then let the current tumble your bait or lure to a waiting fish. Where the water flows strongest, you'll have to squeeze on a split-shot sinker to keep your line from being swept downstream too quickly. Always watch the end of your line in the water. When a trout dashes out from behind a boulder to snatch it, you will see it happen. Trout are the wariest of all fish. If a trout misses grabbing your hook, or it sees the line in the water, the trout will reject it in an instant and zip back to its hiding place to wait and watch for something else it can catch and eat to come drifting by.

Any trout you catch in small cold-water streams will most likely be brook trout — or brookies, as they are commonly called. Brook trout thrive in cool, sun-dappled pools and darkly shaded holes under banks. They cannot tolerate the warmer water of streams that flow in open sunlight. In more brightly lit waters you will find rainbow trout, brown trout, or both. Because warm water is usually richer in food than cold

water, rainbows and browns grow larger than
their brook trout cousins.

Fishing in large streams for big trout requires
casts of twenty to thirty feet and more. Cast your
line upstream at a forty-five-degree angle from
the current and begin retrieving as soon as the
hook hits the water. The flow will carry your line
downstream all during your crosscurrent retrieve,
covering a lot of water and passing many possible
fish-holding spots along the way. Most strikes
occur at the end of each drift as the line suddenly
bows and your lure is swept along in a swift arc.
If no fish takes on this downstream swing, you
simply keep retrieving your lure. The strong

current will add all the action needed to entice fish along the way.

Where currents are strong, fish face into it, keeping their streamlined bodies in line with the water's flow. Aquatic insects, smaller fish, and crustaceans tumble downstream, and the fish watch and wait for food to come to them. When you cast, think of the fish all facing upstream, and work your lure or fly a little more actively as it passes each boulder. Fish often station themselves in the slower current behind large rocks. These fish stations are called boulder pockets. Any bait, lure, or fly moving by a big stream boulder is sure to be inspected and either taken or rejected by the fish in the pocket.

FLY FISHING IN STREAMS

The most abundant sources of food in streams are aquatic insects that live in the water and terrestrial insects that fall in the water. Because

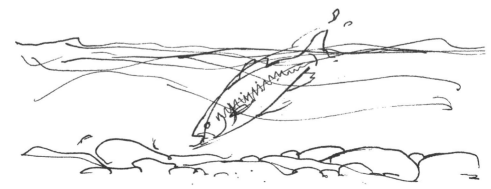

of this, I do almost all of my stream fishing with fly tackle. There are fishing-fly patterns designed to imitate all three stages of aquatic insect life: nymphs, pupae, and winged adults. And there are fly patterns that duplicate the shape and density of various beetles, grubs, ants, caterpillars, bees, grasshoppers, crickets, leafhoppers, and spiders that, for one reason or another, land in the soup.

Some Freshwater Fishing Flies

Sinking or "wet" flies imitate swimming insects.

Buoyant or "dry" flies imitate floating insects.

The tiniest flies imitate mosquitoes, gnats, and midges.

Big flies called "streamers" imitate minnows.

For big streams where trout feed on minnows as well as insects, there are streamer flies that look and move like minnows when retrieved.

A fly will drift more slowly in the water than a heavy lure. Fish get a longer look and have more time to be tempted into striking.

Where the stream bottom is firm, I wade out a little way to cast without interference from shoreline trees. A few false casts is usually all it takes to get enough line in the air to send your fly out to good, fish-holding pockets. Always cast a fly upstream and let it float or drift downstream. Watch the swing at the end of the drift, and retrieve it upstream by stripping in line six or eight inches at a time.

When fishing a pool, try to approach from downstream so the fish facing upstream will not see you. Then fish the entire pool, beginning with the shallow tailwaters, work to the deep center, and finally cast right into the falls at the pool's head. Always keep a firm stance in the water, especially after you've hooked a fish. Bring it to you—don't wade toward it. There are

bound to be channels of deep water carved out by the volume of water. And the wet boulders or ledges around a pool tend to be very slippery. Never wade where the bottom is or looks muddy. Stay out of water that is murky and unclear. Even where the bottom is firm under your step, do not wade deeper than your knees. This is how I fish streams, and I find I can always get my fly wherever I want to cast it.

In rivers, small or large, the currents are usually much stronger than they appear. Look for a safe place onshore to fish from. Stay away from the edges of overhanging banks. Don't walk too close to any rushing currents. Even firm sand near a fast current can quickly give way under the weight of your step. Sometimes the only safe way to fish a river is from a solid bank using spinning tackle that will enable long, pinpoint casts. Reel quickly, though, or your lure will sink and snag on the river bottom.

When you reel a bright, flashy spinner over or alongside a big river boulder, you never know what fish might be lurking behind it. There are lots of other river-dwelling fish besides trout.

CLINCH
KNOT

WIRE
LEADER

Pike, muskellunge, smallmouth bass, eel, salmon, and shad are also caught in rivers. In coastal rivers—where fresh water mixes with salt water—you may hook in to a saltwater species such as a striped bass, redfish, snook, jack crevalle, tarpon, or even a shark! When I fish any water that connects to the sea, I add a four-foot length of twenty-pound test monofilament to serve as a shock tippet. To take the initial power of the strike, a twenty-pound test shock tippet, combined with a full reel of twelve- or seventeen-pound test monofilament, should be enough to handle most fish.

Some fishermen use commercially prepared wire leaders to absorb the strike of a big fish. You can buy wire leaders in various lengths with snap swivels already attached to them. Whether you choose to use heavy monofilament or a wire leader as your shock tippet, you'll be glad you had it when a big, sharp-toothed fish bites.

DON'T FORGET TO BRING A CAMERA SO SOMEONE CAN TAKE A PICTURE TO RECORD THE FISH THAT YOU CATCH AND RELEASE. HERE I AM WITH MY BIGGEST BOWFIN EVER. THE JAW CLAMP, CALLED A FISH GRIP, IS THE ONLY SAFE WAY TO HOLD THIS SHARP-TOOTHED FISH BY THE MOUTH.

SALTWATER FISH AND FISHING

I pinched myself to see if I was dreaming. It was February. Our home in Vermont was socked in with ice and snow. And here I was shielding my eyes from the bright tropical sun of the Florida Keys, looking out at a beautiful blue-green sea. The tide was very low. I was able to wade out one hundred yards without wetting my knees. The water was crystal clear. White sandy patches in the bottom appeared to be floating on the water surface. There were lots of fish. I could see their dark shapes swimming in the shallow water and I spotted their fins sticking up out of the water. Big, silver-sided barracuda splashed on the surface as they chased schools of leaping mullet. Whole squadrons of jack crevalle raced by, creating their own wave in the otherwise waveless water. And bonefish hovered

ghostlike over brownish beds of turtle grass.
All of the fish were extremely wary and
easily spooked because they could see
me through the clear, shallow water.
I waded slowly, placing each step firmly but
carefully, trying not to disturb the powdery
crushed coral bottom.

A small stingray, which had been buried in
the powder waiting to ambush some unfortunate
prey, suddenly scooted out from under my step.
I stopped right there and made my first cast. My
spinning tackle gave me all the distance I needed
to reach the various dark patches of turtle grass
and seaweed where big fish tend to hang out.
I was using a new lure called a cuda tube, which
consisted simply of eight inches of plastic
surgical tubing pulled over a length of strong,
braided wire. According to the fellow at the bait
shop, all you need to do to fish a cuda tube is
cast it as far as you can and reel it back as fast
as you can. That's exactly what I did and
right away I had a whole pack of barracuda
following the lure.

CUDA TUBE

I wasn't so sure I wanted all those sharp-toothed barracuda racing toward me and my bare legs, but I kept reeling anyway, as fast as I could crank the handle. The gang of fish chased the bright green tube until, all at once, they spotted me and instantly veered away. I was both disappointed and relieved. I raised the rod to lift the lure out of the water and cast again, this time a little farther out. The plop of the heavy lure on the waves got the attention of a cruising cobia, and the big fish turned in the water to give chase just as I began my retrieve. The cobia came on strong, approaching the lure's big hooks so closely, I was sure it would bite. But, just as the barracuda had done, this fish suddenly veered away.

My heart was throbbing. The cobia had come so close, I could see its distinctive black and white stripes. It was bigger than any freshwater fish I had ever seen, let alone hooked. All of the fish that chased the lure were big fish. All were spooked at the very last second before biting because they spotted me through the ultra-clear water.

I was wading to a new spot, following the edge of an immense submerged meadow of turtle grass, when I came upon a fish that wasn't afraid of me at all. I saw the shark's tail first as it waved slowly in the water. From a distance of less than fifteen feet, I stared at the spot until I could make out the whole fish — big, upright dorsal fin; gill slits pumping; black beadlike eyes in a wide, flattened head. The shark was swimming very slowly. When it suddenly settled down on a bar of bright sand between two dark weed beds, I realized it was a nurse shark and it was scouring the bottom for crabs. Nurse sharks are not aggressive unless touched or grabbed. And because so many snorkelers do just that, nurse sharks account for 90 percent of all shark bites. I wasn't going to touch this shark. Very slowly, I backed away, giving myself and the shark more space. At twenty-five feet I felt completely safe and could still see the shark clearly. With fishing rod tucked under my arm, I pulled out my little notepad and made a quick drawing of the shark,

noting its rich, reddish brown color and the deep folds of skin around each of its fins. As I was making notes, the shark gently rose off the sandbar and swam away.

When I resumed fishing, my fishing was better. The shark sighting made me even more watchful, and I began spotting fish to cast to at even greater distances. I also had learned to crouch a little to change my human shape when fish were near. When a pack of four big barracudas raced after my lure, I crouched lower and lower, reeling as fast as I could until one of the fish smashed the hooks! From that point on I hooked and lost fish after fish — barracuda, needlefish, triggerfish, and puffers. It was all the action that saltwater fishers dream of.

But the high point of the day was the quiet time I spent watching the shark and the realization that, while the fishing methods for salt water are essentially the same as those used in fresh water, fishing for saltwater fish is by its very nature something altogether different. There are freshwater fish that can prick or stab you with a barb, and some freshwater fish bite. But there are no freshwater fish that can fatally

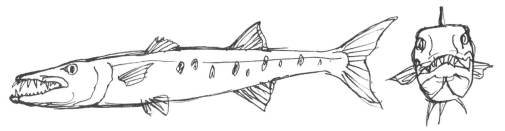

wound you or bite you in half. Saltwater fish, on
the other hand, can be powerful and potentially
dangerous.

When I spotted the nurse shark, I was
standing in less than eighteen inches of water.
The water was clear. I saw the shark clearly.
The shark could see me. I was quite safe. Had
the water been murky or clouded by breaking
waves, I would not have waded in. Stingrays and
sharks need very little depth to swim. And your
only safety in waters where these fish live is your
ability to see bottom all around you for a radius
of at least fifty feet.

Recently, from the safety of shore, I watched
a great hammerhead shark attack and kill
a tarpon in water only five feet deep.
The tarpon was large, more than
one hundred pounds.

55

The hammerhead was a monster. Its dorsal fin was two feet high. Five feet of water surface separated the dorsal fin from the tail fin. I estimated the shark to be over twelve feet long and to weigh close to seven hundred pounds. It struck the tarpon repeatedly, chasing the wounded fish many times before finishing it off in one terrible thrashing, splashing moment. Then suddenly the water was calm and serene again.

The ocean is a vast underwater wilderness as wild near shore as it is in its depths. Fish in the ocean have a universe of open water to cruise and hunt in, and when they themselves are being hunted or chased, they have a world of water to flee in. Most ocean species are streamlined for speed. Many have sharp teeth to latch onto speedy prey. Fish that feed on slow-moving crustaceans and shellfish are equipped with powerful, crushing jaws. There is a lot of chasing, chomping, and crunching going on in salt water.

Saltwater Fish

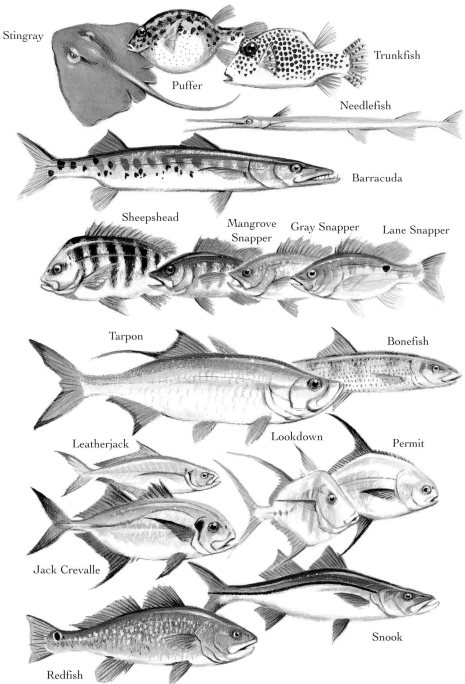

Stingray

Puffer

Trunkfish

Needlefish

Barracuda

Sheepshead

Mangrove Snapper

Gray Snapper

Lane Snapper

Tarpon

Bonefish

Leatherjack

Lookdown

Permit

Jack Crevalle

Snook

Redfish

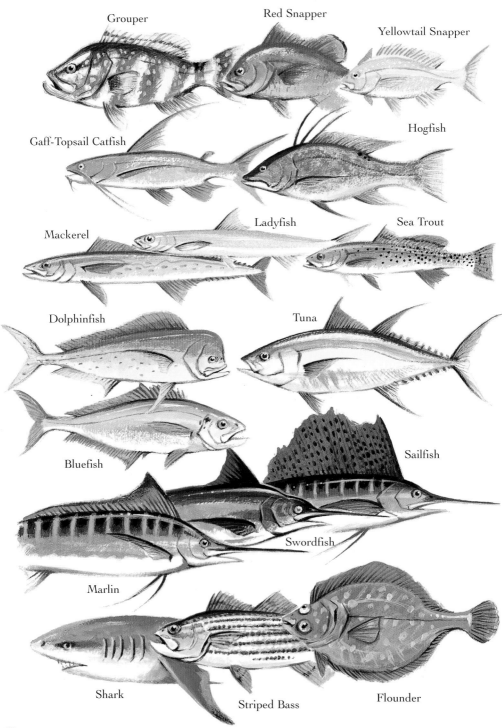

Grouper

Red Snapper

Yellowtail Snapper

Gaff-Topsail Catfish

Hogfish

Mackerel

Ladyfish

Sea Trout

Dolphinfish

Tuna

Bluefish

Sailfish

Swordfish

Marlin

Shark

Striped Bass

Flounder

Saltwater Places to Fish

WITH LITERALLY OCEANS OF SALT WATER TO FISH IN, WHERE DOES A FISHERMAN START?
HERE ARE SOME SALTWATER PLACES WHERE YOU CAN TRY YOUR LUCK.

Estuary

ESTUARIES ARE FRESHWATER RIVERS THAT FLOW
INTO THE SEA. FISH THEM AS YOU WOULD ANY
FRESHWATER RIVER OR CREEK.

Docks and piers

FISH CONGREGATE IN THE SHADE BENEATH
DOCKS AND PIERS.

Surf

SURF FISHING REQUIRES A LONG, POWERFUL ROD
TO CAST HEAVY SINKERS AND BAIT INTO THE
BREAKING WAVES.

Flats

THE FLATS ARE SHALLOW-WATER AREAS WHERE
THE WATER IS ONLY A FEW INCHES TO A FEW FEET
DEEP. FLATS FISHING CAN BE VERY EXCITING
BECAUSE YOU CAN SEE THE FISH COMING TO
YOUR LURE OR BAIT.

Channels and bays

WHERE THE CURRENTS ARE SLOW, CHANNELS
AND BAYS ARE FISHED THE SAME WAY YOU FISH
STILLWATER PONDS OR LAKES.

To ward off hungry predators, many small fish have sharp barbs or stingers that can inflict painful wounds. A fisherman catching and unhooking any saltwater species must take great care to protect his fingers, hands, and arms.

Saltwater fish locate food by smell more than by sight. They roam the water endlessly searching for the scent of fish in distress or blood oozing from a wound. A single drop of blood can trigger a feeding frenzy. If you draw any blood hooking and landing a fish in salt water, you might as well kill it and eat it yourself (if it is edible), because it won't last an hour in the merciless sea. I learned this the hard way. While fishing from shore, I caught a two-pound needlefish and played it along the water's edge to where I could show it to my wife, Deanna. We were admiring the long-snouted fish when I noticed that it was bleeding a little from one gill. Thinking I should get it back in the water quickly so it could recuperate, I waded in and released it by gently letting it swim from my

hands. The needlefish hadn't
gone a distance of three feet when
suddenly the water all around it exploded with
the violent splashing and slashing of a large
barracuda. The barracuda had followed the scent
of needlefish blood and was circling in the
shallows. My careful release of one fish turned
into something like hand-feeding another! I'm
not telling you these stories to frighten you. But
before you go fishing in salt water, you need to
know what kind of realm you are casting into.

FISHING THE SURF

Just a little way off every sand
beach, under the breaking waves, the
constant churning of the water creates
a gully, or trough, in the ocean floor.
These gullies can parallel the shoreline for miles.
Small fish follow this thoroughfare, feeding on
pieces of shellfish, crab, shrimp, and squid
tumbling in with the waves. Large predators swim

the trough feeding on the small fish. I have seen
whole pods of dolphin feeding in a trough so
close to shore that the dolphins pursued their
prey right onto the wet beach, wriggling back in
the water with their catch.

Surf fishermen know about the gullies, and
use long, powerful rods to cast their baited hooks
out to the busy gully. A heavy pyramid-shaped
sinker quickly drops through the waves and digs
into the sandy bottom to hold the line and bait in
place. Depending on the beach, the gully may be
as close as fifty feet from shore and surf casters
need only lob their bait over the nearest breaking
wave.

Weakfish, channel bass, black drum,
pompano, sea robin, striped bass, stingray, shark,
bluefish, mackerel, flounder, fluke, barracuda,
tarpon, sheepshead, and croaker are all fish that

can be caught in the surf. Favorite surf fishing baits are bloodworms, small soft crabs, shrimp, chunk-cut mullet, and strips of squid. When bait is used, you can cast, prop your rod in the sand, sit down, and relax. Watch the tip of your rod. If it dips and rises rhythmically, it is only the waves pulling your line. If it jerks, you have a fish nibbling your bait. If the rod is yanked down hard, you have a fish on.

SURF ROD HOLDER

SAFE, DRY AREAS ON JETTIES ARE ALSO GOOD PLACES FROM WHICH TO FISH THE SURF.

The benefit of using natural bait, such as minnows or bloodworms, in surf fishing is that fish can smell it. Scent is the best way to get your bait noticed amid all the other foods swirling and tumbling around in the foam. If you prefer to use lures, use big spoons, large splashy plugs, or big bushy flies with tinsel tied in them for sparkle in the water. Depending on the artificial bait you use, your tackle will vary. But the basics of saltwater fishing are the same. Cast out to the gully, and as soon as your lure or fly hits the water, begin retrieving. If you don't catch a fish on the first dozen casts, try varying your retrieves—reeling slower or faster or in short jerks. Cast to different spots. Cast a little farther out. Cast where there are gulls or pelicans on or over the water. Birds mean baitfish, and these small fish attract bigger fish. Once you get a fish

Surf fishing rig with pyramid sinker to hold bottom in waves

Two bait hook-ups

on, jerk the rod backward once or twice to embed the hook, then keep your line tight and stand your ground. Reel until the rod lowers and then pull it strongly until it is upright before reeling in again. This pumping action is the best way to pull a fish to you.

Fish caught in the surf can be landed easily by sliding them onto the wet beach. There, a fish can be safely unhooked and kept, or released with a gentle nudge with your foot or rod-butt back into the sea.

To hold a fish, grasp it around the base of the tail. I carry a rubber-coated glove for grasping slippery fish, pulling the glove out of my pocket and slipping it on just before I reach for the fish in the water. If my fish escapes before I get the glove on, all the better. As always, sharks or rays are cut loose, untouched. Use long pliers (not your fingers) to unhook fish. If you catch a stingray, watch out for that barbed tail! Use your pliers to cut the line close to the fish's mouth and let the stingray go. The salt in the water will soon corrode the hook and it will fall away on its own.

Once subdued, even large barracuda can be unhooked safely using pliers.

Sharks—small or not—should never be touched with hand or foot. Sharks are very limber creatures and can bend to bite a hand that is holding them by the tail. If you catch a shark, stand clear of the animal, cut your line at least two feet away from the hook, and let the shark squirm away on its own.

Fishing requires that you use common sense. Be careful when releasing any fish so it doesn't hurt you and you don't hurt it. Wear sun block (30+) to protect your skin from harmful rays and prevent sunburn. A hat with a long bill or broad brim will keep your head cool and shade your eyes. Polarized sunglasses will enable you to see through the glare on the water to the fish below. And a pair of wading shoes will protect your feet from broken seashells or sharp pieces of coral. Carry plenty of water and drink it in small gulps so it will last all day. Keep your fishing line and hooks well away from people. And at the end of the day, rinse your tackle with fresh water to wash away the salt. Salt corrodes metal. Just a gentle freshwater rinse will keep your rod guides from corroding and your reel working smoothly.

You can pick up seashells and admire them. If they are still inhabited, however, always put them back where you found them.

FISHING BOTTOM TO TOP

The baits for bottom fishing are the same as baits used in fishing the surf. People who fish the bottom like to use multiple hooks on one line to present baits at different depths. And they prefer rounded sinkers that will drag on the bottom and allow their bait to drift a little. The rods used for bottom fishing in salt water are short and stiff enough to haul heavy fish up from depths of fifty feet or more.

Most bottom fishing in salt water is done from piers, bridges, or boats. There is little or no casting. Bait is simply lowered to the ocean floor. Since most bottom-dwelling fish are good to eat, there is very little releasing. Flounder, codfish, pollack, halibut, grouper, sea bass, and snapper are all fish taken from the depths and brought home to the freezer.

If you do release a fish from the height of a pier or bridge, drop the fish headfirst so it reenters the water as smoothly as possible and will not be stunned or injured by the impact.

A GOOD BOTTOM FISHING RIG HAS TWO BAIT HOOKS AND AN EGG SINKER THAT DRAGS ON THE BOTTOM, MOVING THE BAIT WITH THE EBB AND FLOW OF THE CURRENTS.

Experienced saltwater fishermen fish the changing tides, when the tide is flowing in or flowing out. At those times, there are more fish traveling in the water. They swim in with the high water to feed in the food-rich bays, and they leave as the tide begins to flow back out.

Out on the jetties or in channels and canals where the water is always deep enough for big fish, a floating lure drifting in the slow current and then retrieved in short, splashing jerks can produce surprising strikes from small grunts and snappers to great, big jacks. On the southern coast of the United States, where I do much of my saltwater fishing, a lure or fly cast close to mangrove roots can bring a big snook or redfish out of hiding or tempt a nearby tarpon into striking.

You cast and retrieve the flies used for saltwater fish the same way you do freshwater flies. The only difference is that saltwater flies tend to be much bigger and more wind resistant than most freshwater flies. You need a stiff and powerful fly rod to whip these big flies out over the water. And you

Some Saltwater Fishing Flies

Crab imitation

Two shrimp imitations

Three baitfish imitations

WHEN WADING, FLY FISHERMEN CARRY ALL THEIR GEAR ON THEM. I USE A LANYARD TO CARRY MY FLY BOXES, LEADER MATERIAL, SCISSORS, AND HOOK SHARPENER.

Note: All flies are shown actual size.

need a reel large enough to hold your fly line and at least four hundred yards of fifty-pound test backup line. Saltwater fish run and run and run. If you don't have enough line to give them, they'll take what you have and your fishing rod, too!

I have felt the powerful run of a saltwater fish most spectacularly in the extremely shallow, even-bottomed coastal waters known simply as "the flats." Flats fishermen move stealthily, looking for signs of their quarry in the shallow water: a cloudy spot where a bonefish is grubbing on the bottom for crabs; a sudden wake created by the back of a permit or jack racing by; tarpon tails or dorsal fins sticking up out of the waves; or the long shadow of a nearly invisible barracuda on the sandy bottom. All of these signs are clear in water no deeper than twelve inches. And the fish are fish that can outweigh the fishermen!

The flies for fishing the flats are made in patterns that imitate the colors, shapes, and sizes of shrimp, crab, and small baitfish. When I fly fish the flats, I wade no deeper than my knees—and only in crystal-clear water, so I can see the fish I'm casting to and watch out for stingrays underfoot.

Another way to fish the flats is from shore, using spinning tackle to cast out to feeding fish or weed beds where fish may be. Lures, such as surface plugs, that sputter and chug, silver spoons that wobble and flash, big, buck-tailed spinners that whir and buzz through the water, and those long cuda tubes all work well on the flats.

No matter what method of fishing you use on the flats, when you hook a fish, the first thing you must do is let the fish run. Spin fishermen, remember to set your drag to pull slowly off the spool. Your fish is going to make a beeline for deep water. You won't be able to begin reeling until the fish pulls out enough line so that the weight of it dragging in the water will turn the fish around. Eighty feet of heavy fly line and hundreds of feet of backup line will eventually slow any fish down. Once this happens and you feel the slack, reel like mad. If the fish runs again, stop reeling and let it run until the process is repeated.

WATCHING OUT
FOR STINGRAYS

If you are fly fishing and you hook up, you are in for a thrill. Your eighty feet of fly line will appear to vaporize off the reel. Then, as you watch your backup line peeling away, there will be nothing you can do but hold on. Keep your finger away from the reel handle as it rotates at high speed, feeding the line out. When you sense a halt, retrieve all the line you can before the fish rockets away again. A fly rod designed for salt water has a soft rubber ball molded onto the butt end to cushion the rod against your stomach during a fish's powerful run. Wedge that rod-butt on your belt and hold on. You will see your rod bend nearly in two, and if you don't give the fish line, the rod will snap. After many runs and leaps, your fish will tire and be ready for reeling in.

It is a long way from the sunfish ponds of my boyhood to the blue green waters of warm southern seas. This distance isn't measured in miles but in casts and line reeled in, fish caught and fish lost, and water covered. I have made my journey from freshwater to saltwater fishing by respecting the marine environment, learning all I can about the species of fish I may encounter, and always keeping my own safety in mind. I've

fished flats, channels, canals, bridges, jetties, banks, piers, and surf. I've ventured miles offshore seeking bluefish in the North Atlantic and sailfish in the Florida Straits. Saltwater fishing has taught me more about our watery planet than any book or TV show or CD-ROM could. And best of all, when I cast my line into the sea, I become a very real participant in the drama and life of Earth's first and last great wilderness.

CRAYFISH ON ITS MOORING IN THE SPARKLING WATERS OF LAKE CHAMPLAIN

PART II
BOATING

*Believe me, my young friend, there is nothing —
absolutely nothing — half as much worth doing
as simply messing about in boats.*

Water Rat, KENNETH GRAHAME, *THE WIND IN THE WILLOWS*

I know exactly what Water Rat meant. I have
spent whole days doing nothing more than
messing about in my boat, *Crayfish*. I mop and scrub
and polish. I sweep and brush. I coil and fold and
neatly stow. I rearrange. I start the engine, let it run,
then shut it off. I clean and wipe. I pump the bilge. I
count my hours aboard the boat — under way or just
afloat — the way a miser counts newly minted coins.

Out on the water, everything on land seems far
away. Your boat becomes an island unto itself with
a singular view of the world and a language all its
own. Floor becomes deck. A ceiling is a cover.
Walls are bulkheads. Stairs are ladders. Downstairs
is below. Upstairs is topside. The front and back of
the vessel are fore and aft. Facing forward, the left
is port. Right is starboard. (To remember which is
which, I think of the words *port* and *left* each
having four letters.)

On a boat, rope is not called rope. It is line. A door is a hatch. A window is a hole. A storage box or closet is a locker.

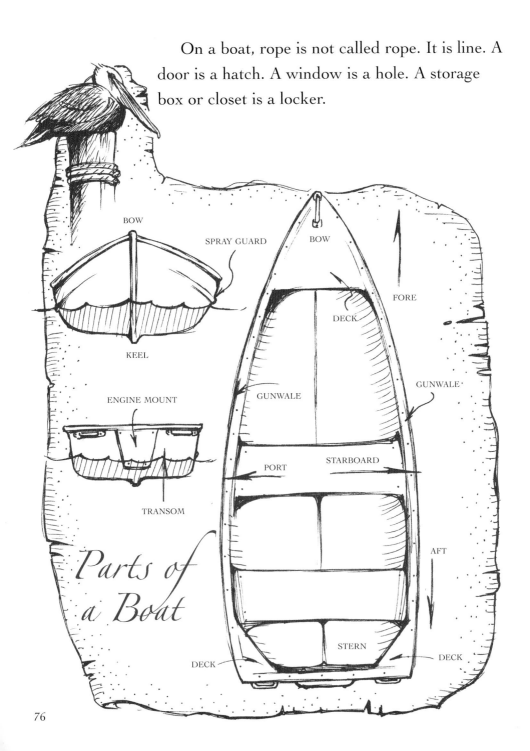

BOW

SPRAY GUARD

BOW

FORE

DECK

KEEL

ENGINE MOUNT

GUNWALE

GUNWALE

PORT

STARBOARD

TRANSOM

AFT

Parts of a Boat

DECK

STERN

DECK

TO A BOAT LOVER, EVERY BOAT—LARGE OR SMALL,
IN THE WATER OR OUT ON SHORE—IS A THING OF BEAUTY.

U.S.S. *HANK*

When you are on a boat, experiences add up quickly. There is so much to do and see and wonder about. My memories of time spent onboard are vivid and filled with details. The very first boat I stepped foot on was a great, big boat named *Hank*. I was a nineteen-year-old U.S. Navy seaman. *Hank* was an old World War II vintage destroyer. I was stationed on *Hank* for a training cruise that would take me and 384 other sailors from the Philadelphia Naval Shipyard to the island of Bermuda. Somewhere off the coast of North Carolina we ran into a terrific storm. For safety, all of the sailors except those who navigated and controlled the ship were confined belowdecks. *Hank* was tossed around like a small stick out on the ocean. After the storm, we who had been belowdecks emerged and saw that the waves had washed over even the highest parts of the ship. Flying fish, stranded by the storm, were flipping and flopping on the ship's stern.

We reached Bermuda on a bright, sunny morning. For three glorious days I got to explore on foot, photographing colorful cottages, busy fishing docks, the ruins of an old fort, lush tropical gardens, windswept meadows, horses, dogs, birds, and people.

The cruise back was blessedly calm. On the night of my bridge watch, I walked the metal catwalk around the ship's pilothouse, dressed warmly in a wool cap and snug navy sweater. Inside, officers and chiefs were huddled over their charts. The room glowed blue from the light on the chart table. Raising my binocular, I scanned the dark horizon. Suddenly the moon, which had been hidden by clouds, shined through and cast its glow across the ocean. It was water and moonlight as far as the eye could see. Phosphorescent waves rolled up in endless succession. *Hank* plowed through them noiselessly.

Hank was 376 feet long and made of heavy metal, yet it floated like a cork! Any boat, big or small, that has a deep hull (the part of the boat that sits in the water) will float well as long as

DISPLACED WATER

ROUND BOTTOM

FLAT BOTTOM

V-SHAPED

DEEP
V-SHAPED

the overall weight of the boat is less than the weight of the water being displaced (pushed away by the boat's being in the water). *Hank's* hull displaced 3,218 tons of water. So *Hank* must have weighed less than 3,218 tons.

How much water a boat displaces depends not only on the size but also on the shape of the boat's hull. Deep V-shaped hulls displace a lot of water. Boats that push more water out of the way go slower than boats that push less water. Warships, tankers, freighters, barges, ferries, tugboats, fishing trawlers, sailing ships, and large rowboats all have deep hulls. They are the slowest vessels on the water.

Boats with shallower hulls displace very little water and are the fastest boats. Bass boats, runabouts, ski boats, and all other boats built for speed do not plow through water. They skim over it as fast as their engines can make them go. But because they are heavier than the water they displace, such boats need air chambers or some floatation material built in to keep them from sinking.

My own boats have been many and varied. Besides *Crayfish*, which is a mini cabin cruiser, there is a little rubber raft named *Musquash*, a cedar-strip canoe named *Musquash II*, a heavy aluminum rowboat we call *Old Blue Oars*, an aluminum johnboat dubbed *Sneaky Pete*, and *Leeky Teeky*, our inflatable dinghy. I've also owned a live-aboard sailboat, which I christened *Mayfly*. My boats have been my teachers. All I know about boating I have learned from them. Now they and I will teach you!

MUSQUASH

After the navy, I wanted a boat of my own. By then I was a husband and a father. Any boat I bought would have to be big enough to hold me, Deanna, and our two-year-old daughter, Michelle.

And yet it needed to be compact to be stored in our small apartment. The little rubber boat seemed ideal. I named it *Musquash*—a Native American word for muskrat—because it moved along so slowly in the water, bumping its soft nose into lilies and reeds very much the way real muskrats do. *Musquash* is a seven-foot-long, yellow, inflatable rubber lifeboat. It has rubber oarlocks for two tiny aluminum oars. It has two sling-style rubber seats, and a soft rubber bottom that undulates with the water.

We had a lot of fun in *Musquash* exploring placid ponds and slow-moving creeks. I used the little rubber boat for fishing. Deanna and Michelle used it as a swim platform. Then one day I put *Musquash* and my family in a stream that was much too wide and swift. Before I could get the tiny oars going, *Musquash* was pulled into the strong current and swept downstream. The little rubber doughnut of a boat twirled round and round as I rowed like mad trying to gain control. But my strokes were no match against the powerful flow. Finally, *Musquash* grounded on a sandy shoal, where I was able to climb out to pull the boat safely to shore. My legs were shaking.

My heart was racing. Deanna was frightened and could barely speak. Michelle liked the ride so much, she asked if we could do it again.

Musquash taught me an important lesson: The smaller your boat, the less control you may have over it in strong currents or winds and when the water gets choppy or downright mean. *Musquash* is a life raft designed primarily to float and drift. It can be rowed, but only very slowly. And its soft rubber bottom made it very difficult for me to maneuver or for it to track straight in the water.

After that one terrifying ride, we never used *Musquash* in any water that wasn't still and calm. And in any small boat, no matter how graceful and maneuverable it may be, I follow Ben Franklin's advice: "Vessels large may venture more, but little boats should keep near shore."

SMALL BOATS ARE FOR
EXPLORING SLOW-MOVING
CREEKS, POKING AROUND
QUIET BACKWATERS, AND
SPENDING WHOLE AFTERNOONS
ON BEAUTIFUL STILLWATER BAYS.

VICTORY BOG IN VERMONT

BACKWATER OF
LAKE MARION
IN SOUTH CAROLINA

SUNSET OVER
FLORIDA BAY

MUSQUASH II

Years of use took their toll on little *Musquash*. Its rubber skin became dry and cracked from the sun, and eventually could no longer hold air. Today it rests in our barn, draped neatly over an empty water trough.

My next boat was a forest green cedar-strip canoe, which I sentimentally named *Musquash II*. But the name never quite fit. A canoe doesn't poke along like a swimming muskrat. *Musquash II* glides smoothly on the water, like a zephyr of wind. It slides over lily pads and slips between tall reeds. The upswept ends of a canoe distinguish it from any other small craft—a canoe is the only boat that smiles at you!

The very first canoes were made from whole tree trunks cut to the desired boat length and then chopped and burned to hollow them out. These canoes were called dugouts. I had seen

Dugout canoe

dugout canoes only in movies or museums. Then one afternoon in the Everglades I saw a dugout canoe resting submerged on the bottom of a dark water pool. Even there, it looked beautiful and evoked adventure.

All slender boats that are tapered fore and aft so they go backward as easily as they go forward are cousins of the canoe.

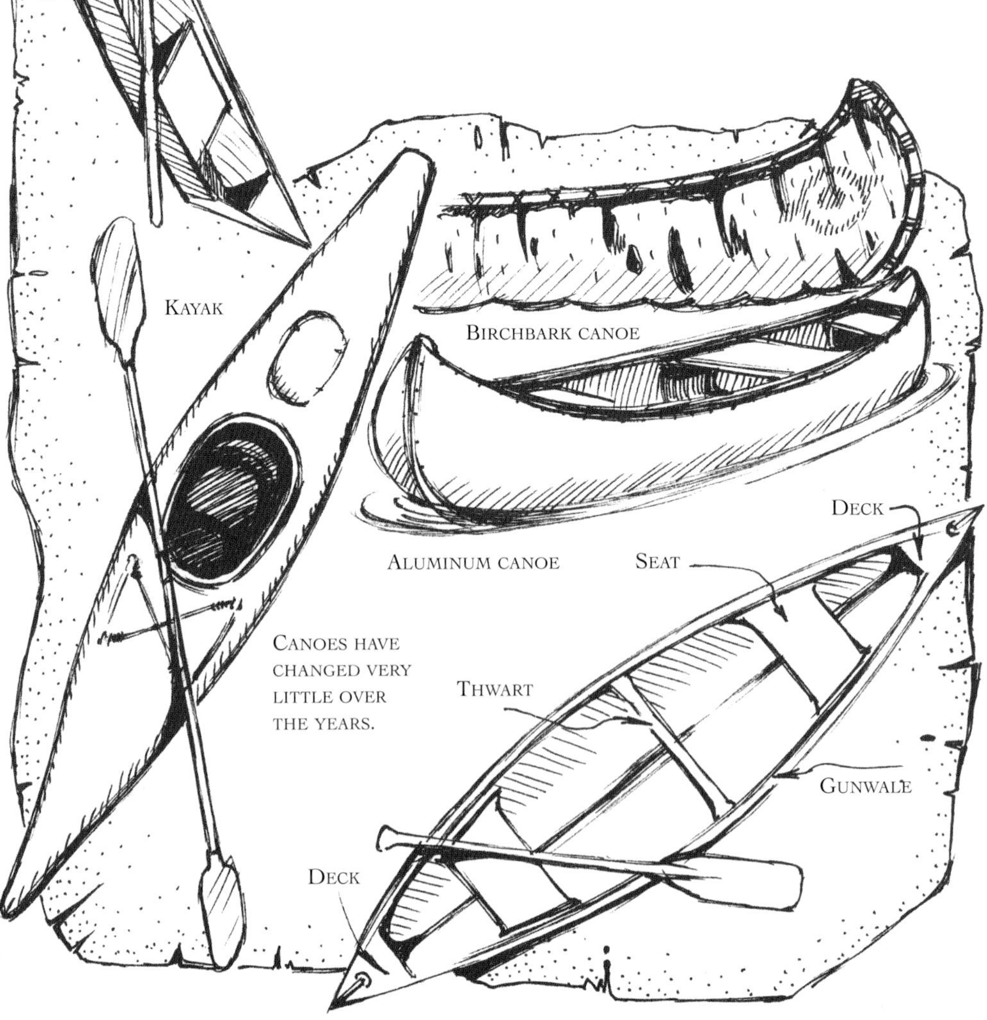

KAYAK

BIRCHBARK CANOE

ALUMINUM CANOE

CANOES HAVE
CHANGED VERY
LITTLE OVER
THE YEARS.

DECK

SEAT

THWART

GUNWALE

DECK

PADDLING A CANOE

The narrow shape of a canoe makes it tippy in the water. When you board a canoe, step in near where the keel runs under the hull. That is the center and the most stable part of the canoe. If you step in too far off center, the boat might tip over. Sit right down and stay put. Never stand in a canoe. Take hold of the paddle, reach it forward over one side of the canoe, and dip the blade quietly in the water. Paddling a canoe should be a silent experience. With the blade at a right angle to the boat, begin to pull the paddle toward you. The canoe will glide forward. At the end of the stroke, turn the blade so it is parallel to the canoe and hold it that way for a few seconds. This acts as a rudder to keep your course straight. Then lift the paddle out of the water to reach it forward and begin another stroke. It's as easy as that!

Paddle on one side of the canoe for as long as you can keep the boat tracking straight. If the bow begins to fall off course, lift the paddle out of the water, over the canoe, and begin your next stroke on the opposite side. The bow will ease back on course.

HERE IS THE PROPER WAY TO HOLD A CANOE PADDLE.

PADDLE ON ONE SIDE FOR AS LONG AS THE BOAT TRACKS STRAIGHT.

To turn, reach the paddle outward away from the side of the canoe and stroke harder until the bow is pointing in the direction you want to go. To turn left, stroke wide to starboard. To turn right, stroke wide to port.

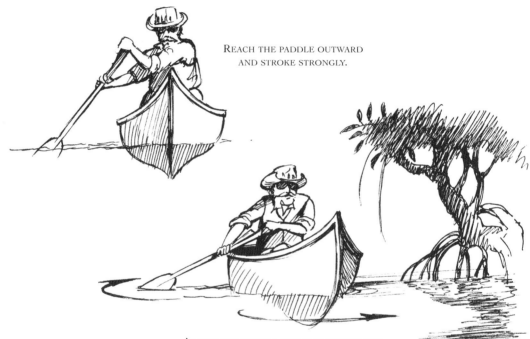

REACH THE PADDLE OUTWARD AND STROKE STRONGLY.

AS YOU STROKE ONE WAY, THE BOW OF THE CANOE WILL TURN THE OPPOSITE WAY.

To slow the canoe's glide, hold the paddle steady in the water at a right angle to the boat. The canoe will gradually slow down and eventually stop.

Because a canoe can float in just a little water, it can go places few other kinds of boats can get to. Deanna and I use *Musquash II* to explore the shallow backwaters of marshes and swamps. There, where the water is often only inches deep, I poke the paddle blade in the water down to the bottom and pole the boat along.

Today, our once shiny new canoe is old and worn and has many leaks, but it still floats. We continue to use it for exploring shallow weedy waters. I have used *Musquash II* for fishing, sketching water animals, and even as a prop on TV! When Vermont ETV produced a PBS series based on my book *Drawing from Nature*, the boat I used on screen was *Musquash II*. The forest green canoe with brown cedar-strip planking was featured prominently in all of our scenes of streams and ponds. In one particular scene I was to paddle all around a beaver's lodge and talk to the viewers as though they were in the canoe with me. What was actually in the canoe with me were the camera, sound recorder, and yards of electronic cables. All this high-priced equipment,

A WHISTLE TIED TO
ANY LIFESAVING
DEVICE INCREASES
THE LIKELIHOOD OF
A PERSON'S BEING
QUICKLY LOCATED
IN THE WATER.

along with our intrepid cameraman, was somehow squeezed into the canoe's foresection while I sat aft. I paddled and talked. The camera rolled. And we got the scene we wanted, all thanks to a leaky old canoe named *Musquash II*.

BOATING SAFETY

A small boat is a confined area. There is no room for horseplay. Fast and jerky movements can rock the hull and cause someone to fall overboard. Move slowly and deliberately. Store tackle boxes and coolers where they can be easily reached and gotten into.

People in the boat should be seated so their weight is distributed evenly to prevent the boat from listing dangerously to one side. Point fishing rods away from faces and eyes. Keep sharp hooks and lures off seats and decks. And when not in use, anchor and dock lines should be safely coiled where they cannot become tangled around feet.

LIFE RING

FLOAT CUSHION

LIFE VEST

IN CASE OF AN EMERGENCY, YOUR BOAT'S ANCHOR CAN HOLD YOU IN PLACE UNTIL HELP COMES.

In a small boat there is no escape from the sun. I always wear a hat when I'm boating. My hat is made of light straw and has a wide brim to shade my face and neck. You can make your boating hat fun to wear by decorating it with seashells or found feathers. I have shiny lures and colorful fishing flies stuck on my straw hat.

To help protect your skin from the sun, apply plenty of sun block. Professional fishermen and boat captains use sun block every time they go out. It doesn't take long for skin to burn badly.

Bring along a bottle of drinking water to prevent dehydration, and a first aid kit with antibiotic cream and a good supply of Band-Aids. There are a hundred ways to accidentally nick and scrape and scratch and cut yourself on a boat.

Finally, boating is not something you should try to learn on your own. To be safe, you need someone with experience onboard. Poll the adults in your family to find out which ones like to go boating and ask if you can go with them. Everyone likes to have a boating buddy. My boating buddy is Deanna. On *Crayfish* she takes the helm and steers when I need to tend to something on deck. With Deanna onboard there are two of us always watching the water for floating debris, buoys, or rocky shoals that could damage the boat. In our smaller boats, Deanna shares the paddling or rowing. Boating buddies are ready to help if one gets hurt or falls overboard. Deanna and I wear our life jackets — but we are each other's best life preservers.

OLD BLUE OARS

I found the old, heavy-gauge aluminum skiff in an auto mechanic's parking lot. The boat was filled to the gunwales with rainwater. An offer, a sale, a short ride home in the back of my truck, and the boat was mine! I named it *Old Blue Oars* after the two faded blue oars that came with it.

In addition to being extremely rugged, *Old Blue Oars* was made with an exceptionally deep V-shaped hull and an unusually broad beam. There was a time when I used *Old Blue Oars* almost exclusively when fishing the big bays of Lake Champlain. The boat's deep hull sliced through the waves, and its broad beam gave it great stability in rough weather. Powered by a four-horsepower outboard motor, *Old Blue Oars* always got me where the fish were.

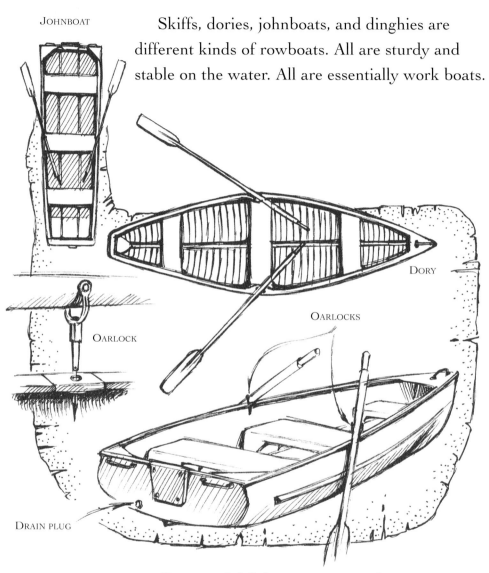

JOHNBOAT

Skiffs, dories, johnboats, and dinghies are different kinds of rowboats. All are sturdy and stable on the water. All are essentially work boats.

DORY

OARLOCKS

OARLOCK

DRAIN PLUG

Commercial fishermen use rowboats to carry supplies and crew to their larger vessels moored

out in deep water. Bait fishermen
use rowboats to net and haul their catch.
The rowboat is still a favorite among bass,
crappie, and walleye fishermen. Special
rowboats designed for drifting and rowing big
rivers are used to fish for trout and salmon.

Waterfowlers pile their decoys, shotguns, and
Labrador retrievers into old reliable rowboats
and head out into the weather to get to their
camouflaged blinds. Some rowboats are actually
used as floating duck blinds. They are
spray-painted with green and brown blotches,
and netted over with cattail-colored mesh.

On the coast, the lifeguard's big, flat-bottomed
dory is a symbol of safety and vigilance.
Lifeguard dories are rowed, not motored, to
swimmers in distress because oars work
instantly. Engines can fail.

ROW, ROW, ROW YOUR BOAT

Rowing a boat is a lot like walking backward.
It seems difficult at first, but with a little
adjustment, you can do it. When you row a boat,

you sit backward, facing the stern. You have to twist around in order to see where you are going. It is lucky that out on the water there aren't too many things to bump into, so you can row and row your boat and twist around only once every three or four strokes to see what's ahead.

In a rowboat the oarlocks hold the oars at the precise angle for rowing. All you have to do is dip the oars in the water and pull. It is pulling both oars through the water simultaneously and with the exact same force that takes skill. And skill comes only from practice.

Let's give it a try! Pretend you are in a rowboat, sitting in the rowing seat and facing the boat's stern. The oars are at rest in their oarlocks, with the blade of each oar hanging down in the water. Grasp the oar handles firmly and push down to lift the oars out of the water.

Now, holding both oars parallel to the water surface, push the handles forward, moving the oars toward the bow. Dip the oar blades in the water, pull the handles toward your chest, and the boat will crawl forward. While the boat is still moving under the momentum of your stroke, push down on the handles to lift the oars out of the water, push the oars forward again toward the bow, and dip and pull them through the water a second time. Keep this up, stroke after stroke, and soon your boat will be moving along smoothly and steadily. Don't forget to twist around every three or four strokes to look where you are going.

To turn, row with only one oar, using your left-hand oar to turn the bow of the boat to the left and your right-hand oar to turn the bow of the boat to the right. To stop, hold both oars motionless in the water!

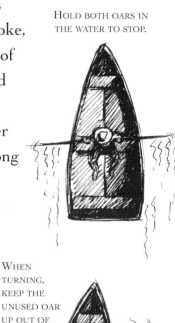

HOLD BOTH OARS IN THE WATER TO STOP.

WHEN TURNING, KEEP THE UNUSED OAR UP OUT OF THE WATER.

DIP OARS IN WATER AND PULL THEM TOWARD THE STERN.

BEGIN WITH OARS OUT OF THE WATER, BLADES TOWARD BOW.

ANCHORING

PLOW-TYPE ANCHORS
ARE DESIGNED TO DIG
IN AND HOLD BOTTOM.

Out on water, all is motion and change. Even on a calm day, a boat moves all the time, dipping ever so slightly as you step or lean over or slide on your seat. The slightest ripple of waves can move a small boat. If you want to stay in one place on the water, you have to anchor your boat to the spot.

There are lots of different styles of anchors. Each is designed to hold in certain kinds of bottoms. But any anchor will keep a small boat from drifting.

What is critical when anchoring any size boat is having enough anchor line. For every foot of depth you are anchoring in, you need seven feet of line. The seven-to-one ratio ensures that your

ANCHOR LINE NEATLY COILED

FASTEN THE
VERY END OF THE ANCHOR
LINE TO YOUR BOAT.

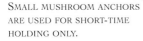

SMALL MUSHROOM ANCHORS
ARE USED FOR SHORT-TIME
HOLDING ONLY.

98

anchor digs into the bottom on an angle that will hold. For example, to anchor in ten feet of water, you let out seventy feet of line plus a few more feet of line for the height of your bow.

Make sure the very end of your anchor line is permanently tied to something sturdy in the boat's bow, such as the bow seat. Then when you anchor, if the knot used to tie off the amount of line in the water happens to slip, you won't lose your anchor and all your anchor line with it. For storage, coil the anchor line neatly in the bow and rest the attached anchor on it.

When anchoring, position the boat upwind or upcurrent a few boat lengths from where you want to be. Then go forward in the boat and lower the anchor. As the boat drifts backward, feed out some line. When you have enough line in the water, fasten the line to the bow ring or cleat. Wait a second or two. Then try pulling the anchor in. If the boat moves toward the anchor, the anchor is holding. If you can drag the anchor to the boat, you have to do it all again and again

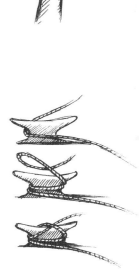

LINE TO BOAT OR DOCK
CLEAT KNOT

until the anchor holds. Once you are anchored, relax and enjoy your own special spot on the water. When you are ready to leave, take hold of the anchor line and pull the boat forward. As you are pulling, coil the wet line neatly in the bow. When you are directly over the anchor, haul it up. It may take a bit of jerking to free it from the bottom. Once the anchor is aboard, carefully remove all weeds and mud. Then rinse the anchor with a dunking or two until it is clean. This will help prevent the spread of unwanted weeds or mollusks from one place to another.

Sometimes it's nice to simply drift. Row a distance into the wind, ship the oars, and let the boat drift back to where you started. For the slowest kind of drift, lower your anchor just enough for it to bounce along on the bottom.

I have spent many wonderful hours adrift. *Old Blue Oars* is as stable as a floating dock. I can stand and cast a fly to all the fishy-looking spots. When I'm not fishing and the drift is slow, I lie back and watch the sky to see if I can make out animals or different kinds of boats in the shapes of passing clouds. If the water is clear, I stare over the side and watch schools of small fish

darting or larger fish taking refuge in the shade
my boat provides. Down on the bottom there are
freshwater clams and mussels creeping, making
long tracks in the sand. Changing my focus, I see
clouds again, reflecting on the water, and I drift
across the lake as if in a dream—sky above,
water below, and *Old Blue Oars* and me
somewhere in between.

THE OUTBOARD MOTOR

Clamped on *Old Blue Oars*'s sturdy transom is
a small, four-horsepower outboard motor. Most
of the time it is not running and is tilted up out
of the water so the propeller (prop) doesn't drag
and slow my rowing. When I want to go
someplace too far for rowing, I lower the prop
into the water and motor to my destination.

PULL-START
ROPE

GAS CAP AND VENT

SHIFT LEVER
FOR REVERSE,
NEUTRAL, AND
FORWARD

R   N   F

TILLER

KILL SWITCH SHUTS
ENGINE OFF

CHOKE GIVES
GAS TO START

TWIST TILLER HANDLE
CLOCKWISE TO GIVE
MORE GAS.

TRANSOM
CLAMP

GAS
COCK

SAFETY CORD ATTACHES TO KILL
SWITCH AND OPERATOR'S CLOTHES
TO STOP ENGINE IN AN EMERGENCY

WATER
COOLING
OUTLET
HOSE

TILT
BRACKET

TO TURN
LEFT

TO GO
STRAIGHT

TO TURN
RIGHT

COOLING WATER INTAKE

PROPELLER

102

A SMALL OUTBOARD ENGINE IS ALL THE POWER A BOAT UP TO 12 FEET LONG NEEDS.

Operating an outboard motor is serious business. Even the tiniest propeller is a dangerous thing when it is spinning. Going fast can be fun, but turning too fast under power can capsize a small boat. Before you try powerboating, you absolutely must take a safe-boating course. In most states, it is required. Even people like me who learned boating before such courses may soon have to pass a safe-boating course. But even after passing a safe-boating course, you will need guidance. Like a pilot learning to fly, you need to get your hours in with Mom or Dad, an experienced older brother or sister, or Uncle Jim before you can be solely in charge. Leave it up to your family to tell you when they think you are ready.

LARGE BOATS NEED MORE POWER. OUTBOARDS FOR BIG BOATS WEIGH AS MUCH AS 700 POUNDS AND ARE AS POWERFUL AS AUTOMOBILE ENGINES.

Under power, you can travel a great distance. But always remember to stay near shore. Your motor may be able to get you where the big boats go, but your small boat will not be safe out there. Near shore doesn't necessarily mean shallow. There may be lots of deep cuts and holes near the shoreline. When you are using a motor, the deeper water is safer water. A powerboater knows the depth of his propeller in the water and diligently avoids water too shallow where striking bottom can damage the propeller.

In environmentally sensitive areas, such as the warm shallow waters surrounding the Everglades National Park, striking bottom or going aground will not only wreck a propeller and leave you stranded, it can harm fragile or endangered marine life. Every year, sea grass, coral, and manatees are accidentally damaged by boat propellers.

IT IS A MOTORBOATER'S RESPONSIBILITY TO WATCH THE BOTTOM DEPTH AT ALL TIMES.

LEEKY TEEKY

What to name a new boat? That's always a serious consideration. Sometimes you think for days about a name. Sometimes you have a name in your mind before you have the boat. And sometimes the perfect name just happens, as in *Old Blue Oars*. I recently bought a new inflatable boat to take with us when we travel. Almost immediately I began referring to the little boat as *Leeky Teeky*, after the old, double-masted schooner in *Adventures in Paradise*, a TV series I watched as a child.

Inflated, *Leeky Teeky* is nine and a half feet long and four and a half feet wide. It has a plywood deck that is divided into sections for storage. A center seat, also inflatable, can be positioned in the middle of the boat when you are rowing, or toward the stern when you are motoring. The sturdy wooden transom can support outboard motors up to ten horsepower.

Inflatable boats have come a long way from the first rubber rafts. Today's inflatables are made of strong denier nylon and they range in overall length from seven to nineteen feet.

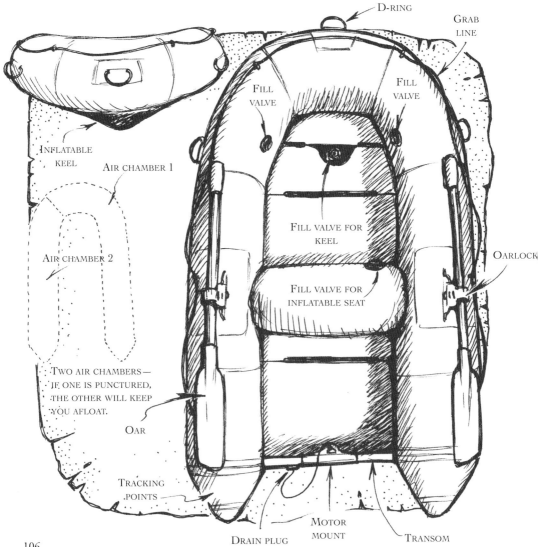

D-RING

GRAB LINE

FILL VALVE

FILL VALVE

INFLATABLE KEEL

AIR CHAMBER 1

AIR CHAMBER 2

FILL VALVE FOR KEEL

FILL VALVE FOR INFLATABLE SEAT

OARLOCK

TWO AIR CHAMBERS — IF ONE IS PUNCTURED, THE OTHER WILL KEEP YOU AFLOAT.

OAR

TRACKING POINTS

DRAIN PLUG

MOTOR MOUNT

TRANSOM

GUNKHOLING

Inflatables are used as dinghies and tenders to larger boats. They are also used in river rapids where, unlike kayaks and canoes, they literally bounce off waves and boulders. And for a type of boating known as gunkholing, an inflatable is the only way to go. Gunkholing is simply drifting in a small boat over shallow water and peering down at the life below. You can go gunkholing wherever the water is shallow and clear and has little or no current.

Deanna and I do most of our gunkholing in the mangrove-lined channels and shallow bays of south Florida. Through crystal clear water we have watched horseshoe crabs, big blue crabs, and spiny lobsters crawling on the bottom. Stingrays almost the size of our boat scoot by. We've seen gangs of dark-backed snook racing after schools of silver mullet. Occasionally, dolphins surface close to our boat.

THE SHADE OF YOUR BOAT ATTRACTS CREATURES.

Leeky Teeky's large, air-filled chambers make great seats to ride on and hang out over in order to watch the water below. And after a dip to cool off or do a little snorkeling, we find the high buoyancy of those air chambers allow us to climb back onboard without fear of capsizing the boat.

One morning on a particularly wonderful gunkholing bay, Deanna and I went snorkeling where we had seen manatees. In less than five feet of depth we saw where the huge animals had been grazing on the sea grass. The manatees had munched wide channels through the tall grass. In some places the grass was nibbled down to the

sandy bottom. Deanna and I held hands and
swam along together, following a clear trail
created by manatees as they ate their way
from one area of the bay to the next.

MANATEE GRAZING GROUNDS

SAILBOATS AT SUNSET IN KEY WEST, FLORIDA

MAYFLY

It all seems like a dream now, but once upon
a time not too long ago I had a sailboat of my
own. It was named *Mayfly*, after the aquatic
insects with upright wings that look like tiny
sailboats on the water. *Mayfly* was twenty-six feet
long and had thirty feet of mast. It was sloop-
rigged, which means it had two sails—a mainsail
(pronounced *mainsil*) and a small forward sail
called a jib.

GAFF-RIGGED

CATBOAT

SLOOP

Sailboats by Shape

YAWL

CUTTER

KETCH

SCHOONER

112

Some sailboats are meant for day sailing. They are little more than a hull with mast and sail. *Mayfly* was a live-aboard sailboat. Belowdecks there was a galley (a small kitchen), a dinette, a head (a bathroom), and a sleeping compartment with two berths (beds). To allow for all this interior space, *Mayfly* had a deep hull. Add to that a full keel, and the boat's draft (the part of the boat that sits in the water) was a little less than five feet. It was a lot of boat for anyone.

It took a lot of practice and much trial and error for me to actually learn to sail *Mayfly*. The fundamentals had to sink in before I fully understood why the boat did the things it did. Just learning the rigging was a challenge.

WEATHERVANE

FORE STAY (SUPPORTS MAST)

MAST

BACK STAY (SUPPORTS MAST)

SHROUD (SUPPORTS MAST)

MAINSAIL

SIDE STAY (SUPPORTS MAST)

BOOM

MAIN SHEET (LINE)

JIB SHEET (LINE)

TILLER

RUDDER

KEEL

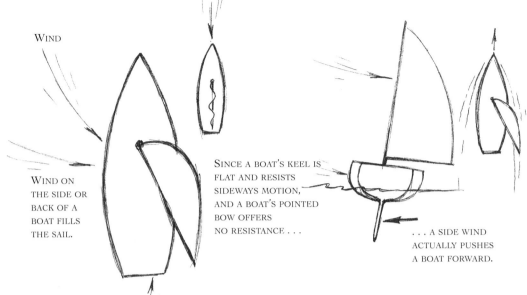

WIND

WIND ON
THE SIDE OR
BACK OF A
BOAT FILLS
THE SAIL.

SINCE A BOAT'S KEEL IS
FLAT AND RESISTS
SIDEWAYS MOTION,
AND A BOAT'S POINTED
BOW OFFERS
NO RESISTANCE . . .

. . . A SIDE WIND
ACTUALLY PUSHES
A BOAT FORWARD.

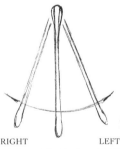

STEER A SAILBOAT TILLER
THE SAME WAY YOU STEER
AN OUTBOARD'S TILLER:

RIGHT   LEFT
TO GO   STRAIGHT   TO GO
LEFT   RIGHT

Any boat can be powered by the wind as long
as it has a sail, a large enough keel, and a bow
narrower than its stern. Without all three, a boat
may float or drift, or be blown downwind, but it
cannot sail. Here's why: When a sail traps wind,
the wind pushes the boat with tremendous force,
which is resisted only by the keel pressing against
the water. The keel prevents the boat from being
blown sideways or knocked down completely.
With all that pressure of wind on sail and water
against keel, something's got to give. What gives is
the boat's hull, which slides in the water, following
the path of least resistance. Since the bow is the
narrowest and least resistant part of the hull, the
boat moves forward. That's sailing!

It sounds simple, but it seemed to take me forever to learn, and I made a lot of mistakes. My first mistake was thinking I could cast off and head out in any direction I wanted to go. In a sailboat you can go where you want to go, but the wind dictates how you will get there. In order to sail into the wind, you have to zig and zag, back and forth across the water. This is called tacking. You tack to starboard, then port, then starboard, and port again, each time gaining a little distance until you complete your passage. A tack may last ten, fifteen, or thirty minutes—and even longer, depending on the wind and the size of the body of water you are crossing. If you are not impatient to get where you want to be, it is a very peaceful and rewarding way to go.

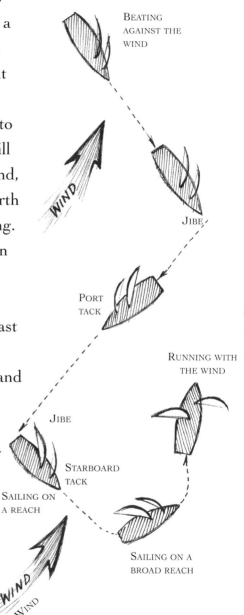

BEATING AGAINST THE WIND

WIND

JIBE

PORT TACK

RUNNING WITH THE WIND

JIBE

STARBOARD TACK

SAILING ON A REACH

SAILING ON A BROAD REACH

WIND

WIND

HERE IS A TYPICAL SAILBOAT COURSE WITH THE FOUR SAILING POSITIONS— BEATING, REACH, BROAD REACH, RUNNING. (IN SAILING, JIBE MEANS TURN.)

There is nothing I have experienced that can compare to the feeling of being out on the water under sail. The only sounds are the lapping of waves against the hull and the occasional snap of the sail trapping wind. Birds flying overhead seem like kin to the boat. The feel of the tiller as it moves the rudder in the water and the gentle heeling over to one side as the boat slices through the waves make sailing the most appealing method of boating. Unfortunately, the activity of sailing that some people handle beautifully and easily became, for me, a chore. I was so busy keeping the boat on course — tacking, jibbing, and trimming the sails to keep them filled with wind — that I could pay attention to little else. I didn't fish. I didn't sketch. I didn't photograph birds. I just sailed. What had begun as a dream of fun and adventure had become something else: a race to get somewhere as fast as the wind and the sails would allow.

Owning *Mayfly* and learning to sail didn't make a sailor out of me. I tried for two whole years. I sailed *Mayfly* on calm water in light breezes. I sailed in thirty-mile-per-hour winds, riding over five-foot-high swells and splashing through deck-soaking waves. And after every outing I had little more to write about in my journal than notes on the weather. Reluctantly I put *Mayfly* up for sale, and happily, it was bought by someone who enjoyed and loved the boat for many years.

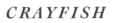

CRAYFISH

I needed a boat as seaworthy as *Mayfly* to take me out on the waves and explore more. But I also wanted to be able to creep the boat into shallow bays and coves to fish and see the wildlife. I wanted to go and come as I pleased, regardless of which way the wind was blowing. My search for the perfect boat ended when I found a uniquely designed mini cabin cruiser built by Arima Boats. I named mine *Crayfish*.

Crayfish is my pride and joy. I call it my
Nature Boat because it is big enough to plow
through waves and get me to the distant islands
where gulls and terns and cormorants nest. And
with the propeller tilted up slightly, *Crayfish*
draws only a foot of water, which means it can
sneak into shallow coves and marshy creeks.

Photos on next page, clockwise: *Crayfish* on its mooring. *Crayfish*'s
cabin and pilothouse. Sunset at Crinkle Cove. Under way. Helm
station. Deanna at the helm. Mosquito netting.

GPS MAP SHOWING *CRAYFISH*'S TRAIL BETWEEN ISLANDS

THE SONAR DEPICTS BOTTOM DETAILS AND FISH.

FLAT BOTTOM, NO FISH

ROCKY BOTTOM. TWO LARGE FISH DEEP, AND SOME SMALL FISH NEAR THE SURFACE

WEED-COVERED HUMP AND LARGE SCHOOL OF FISH

A little over nineteen feet long and nine feet wide, *Crayfish* has a small but comfortable cabin, a roomy pilothouse, and lots of room on deck. A 130-horsepower outboard motor pushes the boat along at a top speed of forty miles per hour. In the stern, there are two tanks for keeping fish fresh for the dinner table or for sketching them later before letting them go. The cabin has space for cameras, big telephoto lenses, snorkeling equipment, notebooks, sketch pads, fishing gear, and a CD player for music out on the water.

I've installed a ship-to-shore radio for emergencies, and a global positioning system (GPS) unit to help me navigate. The GPS receives signals from up to fourteen satellites stationed in the sky that can track a boat's progress. A tiny, three-inch-by-three-inch screen tells me exactly where I am on the globe — latitude and longitude. It also shows me which way I'm headed and keeps me informed of how many miles I've traveled. It even creates a little dotted trail that I can follow back home!

This small but miraculous piece of equipment also features a sonar system that transmits sound waves downward through the water. The sound waves bounce off things—mud, rocks, weeds, even fish—and echo back up to the boat. The viewing screen shows the bounced-back signals in the form of a picture that roughly simulates the lake bottom. Using tiny dots known as pixels, the screen outlines bumps, gullies, and deep holes. It shows fish as tiny fish shapes, one at a time or whole schools together.

"LET'S GO FOR A BOAT RIDE!"

The day was clear and breezy. *Crayfish*—brand-new, fully equipped, and ready to go—bobbed on the water, tugging on its dock lines. With the engine idling in neutral, Deanna cast off the bow line. Then she went aft, cast off the stern line, and said, "Let's go for a boat ride!" I popped *Crayfish* in gear and we headed out on Lake Champlain for our very first cruise. This was

USING MY SONAR AS A GUIDE, I CAN SKETCH THE UNDERWATER WORLD.

Crayfish's "shakedown" cruise, to test the equipment and see how well the boat performed out on the water.

It was slow going in the narrow channel that leads from our cove through two propeller-snagging weed beds and out to deeper water. Once we cleared the weeds, I throttled up the engine and *Crayfish* powered comfortably into the bay. Out in the bay, the air was alive with birds. There were gulls and terns soaring and flapping, riding the breezes and suddenly diving down to the waves. It was a sign that just below the water surface large fish were chasing schools of smaller fish. The gulls and terns were diving and snatching up wounded fish that had floated to the surface. As we approached the highest concentration of bird activity, I glanced at the sonar. The screen showed a dense school of fish directly below us.

MY SONAR SCREEN DEPICTS FISH AS DOTS AND DASHES.
THAT'S HOW I'VE SKETCHED THEM IN THESE UNDERWATER SCENES.

123

We putted steadily along, passing excited birds to our port and starboard sides. I pushed the throttle a little more to pick up speed, causing *Crayfish*'s bow to rise a foot or so in the water. The GPS read ten miles per hour, fifteen, twenty. At twenty-five miles per hour, the bow slowly lowered and the boat evened off in the water. Maintaining that speed, I cruised west for a little more than a mile, slowing down only once to give way to a bass boat approaching my starboard bow. Under what is known on the water as "The Rules of the Road," boats running starboard to other boats have the right of way.

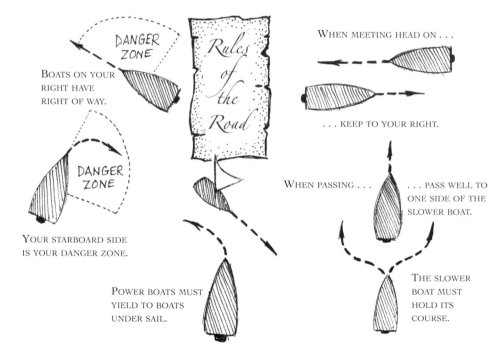

DANGER ZONE

BOATS ON YOUR RIGHT HAVE RIGHT OF WAY.

Rules of the Road

WHEN MEETING HEAD ON . . .

. . . KEEP TO YOUR RIGHT.

DANGER ZONE

YOUR STARBOARD SIDE IS YOUR DANGER ZONE.

WHEN PASSING . . .

. . . PASS WELL TO ONE SIDE OF THE SLOWER BOAT.

POWER BOATS MUST YIELD TO BOATS UNDER SAIL.

THE SLOWER BOAT MUST HOLD ITS COURSE.

We cruised at twenty-five miles per hour due west for another half mile. Then I slowed to a crawl and changed my course, turning sharply into a narrow passage that stretches seven miles to the northernmost waters of the lake. Once in the passage, with miles of deep water below me, I ran the engine full throttle to see how fast we could go. *Crayfish* increased speed until we were scooting along at better than forty miles per hour. That's fast in a boat! "All right!" Deanna exclaimed as our new boat raced the length of the passage, skipping and skimming over the choppy waves.

What Happens When You Throttle Up:

A BOAT GOING SLOWLY IS PLOWING THROUGH THE WATER, USING LOTS OF GAS.

TO RUN FASTER AND USE GAS MORE EFFICIENTLY, A BOAT CAPTAIN INCREASES SPEED UNTIL THE BOAT'S BOW RAISES.

THAT SPEED IS MAINTAINED UNTIL THE BOW SLOWLY LOWERS.

WHEN THE BOW EVENS OFF, THE BOAT IS RUNNING SMOOTHLY OVER THE SURFACE AND NOT PLOWING THROUGH THE WATER.

As we came to the end of the passage, we felt the wind strengthen, blowing hard over a huge, wide-open portion of Lake Champlain known as the Inland Sea. I steered *Crayfish* into the mouth of the Inland Sea and took the wind head-on, bucking three-foot-high waves. The ride was rough but fun, and I kept that windward course for as long as Deanna and I could stand the pounding. Then I eased the boat's bow off the wind and steered *Crayfish* in a wide circle, moving slowly but steadily until the wind was blowing directly on our backs. I next straightened the boat out. *Crayfish* motored smoothly and kept tracking on course while running with the wind on a following sea.

RUNNING WITH THE WIND

BEATING INTO THE WIND

Heading into the wind is always a bumpy ride. But when you are running on a following sea (in the same direction as the wind), you barely feel the motion. There is no water slapping or pounding the hull. You just kind of surf along on the crests of waves. It is a pleasant ride for everyone onboard but the helmsman, because steering a boat with a strong following sea is very difficult. The waves and wind shove and push forcefully against the stern, making the boat sway to port and then to starboard. The bow is constantly veering off course, and you have to work the wheel constantly to make any headway.

WIND ON OUR BEAM (SIDE)

After surfing our way out of the Inland Sea, I turned back into the sheltered water of the passage. Then, following the dotted line on the GPS that had marked the way we had come, I retraced our exact course. The little "bread-crumb" trail on the GPS screen piloted us all the way. It was easy to understand how, at night or in dense fog with no landmarks to help you, the GPS could guide you safely back home.

The next destination on our shakedown cruise was to a special spot we call The Hump. This is a place in the lake where the bottom abruptly climbs from thirty feet to only three feet deep, forming a large, weed-covered knoll. The Hump is a favorite fishing spot, especially at sundown, when bass and pike leave the cooler, deeper water and swim up over the tiny underwater mountain to prowl for sunfish, perch, and minnows hiding in the weeds.

I approached the area slowly, watching The Hump's shape being outlined on my sonar screen. I cruised *Crayfish* into the wind all the way to one end of the huge, submerged knoll. Then with the engine in neutral, and Deanna watching our drift, I went forward and lowered the anchor. The wind and waves drifted *Crayfish* backward over The Hump as I fed out the necessary length of anchor line. With only six feet from our bow to the top of the hump on the lake bottom, I let out seven times six feet to make forty-two feet of line. Then I tugged on the line until I felt the anchor grab and hold firmly in the weedy bottom. As soon as I fastened the anchor line to the bow cleat, *Crayfish*, which had been drifting freely, suddenly swung in an arc on the tight line and held fast, its bow pointing into the wind. We were anchored.

Deanna found a comfortable spot on the foredeck to sit and read and enjoy the sunshine and the breeze. I fished every portion of the weedy water that I could reach with a cast.

ANCHORED ON THE HUMP

The weeds on The Hump grow in columns. On the top of the knoll, the columns are only two or three feet tall. Down the sides of The Hump the weed columns tower eight, ten, and fifteen feet high! Like trees in an underwater forest, the tall weeds are used by predators to hide behind, waiting to ambush passing prey.

The sun was directly overhead, and I could see all the way down into the weed forest. By carefully working a silver spoon lure between the columns, I was able to get a few wildly exciting strikes from large, lurking fish. A long, slender pike rushed out and attacked the lure. And on

another cast, a hefty bass hit it. Each time the fish appeared so suddenly and grabbed the lure so violently, I jerked my rod upward too hard and pulled the lure free.

Another boat was anchored nearby, and a woman onboard caught a bass, which she held up proudly for us to see. Deanna and I applauded appreciatively. When I finally caught a bass of my own, I reciprocated, holding the shining fish high for our neighbors to admire before releasing it back into the shadowy underwater forest.

Wind, waves, boats, and fish filled our afternoon. Whenever a fish or school of fish swam beneath our hull, the sonar chirped Fish! Fish! Fish! Gulls and terns flew by in squadrons. Cormorants snorkeled near the boat and dived under, fishing the same water I fished.

After three hours, I hauled the anchor and we headed back home to our cove. Deanna had things to do onshore. But I wasn't ready to tie up for the day. I dropped her off at the dock and went back out. The wind was blowing harder. The waves in the bay were higher and stippled with sea spray. *Crayfish* sliced through them effortlessly. I hardly felt the water hitting the bow.

The fish seemed invigorated by all the surface motion. In the next two hours I caught fish after fish—perch, bass, and pike. One pike was two and a half feet long and weighed over eight pounds. I used the occasion of its release to finally call it a day. The sun had gone down, and it was getting dark. I could see the masthead lights of sailboats anchored in the distance, and the running lights of boats still under way. I started the engine, turned on my own running lights, and headed *Crayfish* home.

Some Navigational Aids and What They Mean

DAY MARKERS

GREEN "CAN" BUOYS AND
RED "NUN" BUOYS
MARK UNDERWATER HAZARDS.

CHANNEL
MARKERS
GUIDE BOATS
SAFELY
THROUGH
SHALLOW
AREAS.

SLOW DOWN!
YOU ARE ENTERING A
NO WAKE ZONE.

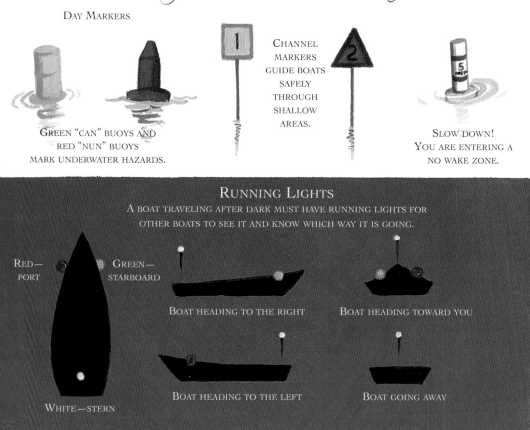

RUNNING LIGHTS

A BOAT TRAVELING AFTER DARK MUST HAVE RUNNING LIGHTS FOR
OTHER BOATS TO SEE IT AND KNOW WHICH WAY IT IS GOING.

RED—
PORT

GREEN—
STARBOARD

BOAT HEADING TO THE RIGHT

BOAT HEADING TOWARD YOU

BOAT HEADING TO THE LEFT

BOAT GOING AWAY

WHITE—STERN

LIGHTED BUOYS MARK THE
ENTRANCE TO A CHANNEL.
GREEN BUOYS—PORT
RED BUOYS—STARBOARD

AT NIGHT, GREEN LIGHT PORT
RED LIGHT STARBOARD

LIGHTHOUSES WARN OF
DANGEROUS REEFS.

EVERY
LIGHTHOUSE HA
ITS OWN PATTE
OF COLOR AND
ITS OWN UNIQU
SEQUENCE OF
LIGHT FLASHES

In our protected cove, the water was still. The air was calm. Scores of blackbirds were flying in for the night to roost in the cattails. I eased in as slowly and quietly as possible so I wouldn't disturb our wild neighbors and, shutting off the engine, coasted up to the dock.

That was the first of many such days of wonder out on the water on *Crayfish*. Like all the boats we've owned and learned from, *Crayfish* offers a quality of experience all its own.

DARREN AND DEREK ON THEIR WAY OUT FOR A DAY ON *CRAYFISH* WITH GRANDPA.

Musquash II and *Old Blue Oars* are still with us. They both rest onshore just a few feet away from the lake. I keep them close enough to the water so they are splashed by waves on windy days. I think they like it. If I were an old boat, I know I would.

When you are boating you are doing something very special. Most people only watch the waves from shore. A boat gets you out to those waves and into the rhythm of their movements. You ride up and over them, feeling the energy of millions of tons of water. When the weather is fair and the water calm, a boat can be the most peaceful place on Earth. You drift over mountains, valleys, gorges, and cliffs that make up the seafloor. And you can probe that mysterious landscape with fishing line, sonar soundings, or your imagination.

COMMON EGRET IN BREEDING PLUMAGE

PART III
WATCHING
WATER WILDLIFE

Sometimes dreams, even those of a fisherman, come true.

ZANE GREY

Because I am a fisherman and boater I have been able to view water and wildlife from vantage points I could not have reached any other way. Wild animals seem unafraid of a fisherman intent only on his line in the water. The sight of geese congregating on rolling waves far from shore, cormorants nesting on treeless islands, or great schools of fish flashing just beneath the water's surface are all things I have seen only from the deck of a boat. My many hundreds of days and thousands of hours on the water have resulted in more than twenty-five books featuring aquatic and semiaquatic animals. And the great diversity of life in rivers, lakes, and in the sea keeps me making new discoveries.

The following pages are all about water wildlife — birds and fish and more. There are charts to help you identify the animals you see, some hints about the behavior of semiaquatic and

aquatic animals, and a special section on the dangerous wildlife you need to watch out for near and in the water.

KEEP THE STRAP SHORT SO THE BINOCULAR RESTS COMFORTABLY AGAINST YOUR CHEST.

USING A BINOCULAR

If you aren't throwing food to them, birds and most other wildlife will keep a distance from you. A binocular brings you close to birds and other animals without frightening them away. Whenever Deanna and I are around water—in boats or even driving in a car—we each carry a binocular to watch the local wildlife.

Using a binocular is the only safe way to get a close-up look at potentially dangerous animals in their natural habitats. Through our binoculars we have watched alligators and venomous snakes and have seen them more closely than we would ever want to actually be.

Every binocular is marked with numbers indicating the magnification power, the diameter in millimeters of each of the two light-gathering lenses, and the field of view at 1,000 yards. For

A RUBBER-ARMORED BINOCULAR CAN TAKE THE BUMPS AND BANGS OF BOATING.

example, a binocular marked "7 X 35/367' at 1,000 yds" has the power to magnify an object seven times, making it appear seven times closer to you than it actually is. Each lens measures 35 millimeters in diameter. And when you are viewing a scene 1,000 yards away, the binocular will show a portion of the landscape 367 feet wide.

The greater the lens power, the more difficult it is to hold a binocular steady. A 10X binocular will exaggerate every tremble of your hands. If you cannot hold the binocular rock steady, it may be impossible for you to clearly see what you are focusing on. For wildlife watching, where a binocular often is held up to the eyes for long periods of viewing, the magnification should be no greater than 8X but no lower than 7X. The binocular Deanna and I recommend is a 7.5 X 42. The extra-large 42-millimeter lenses gather plenty of available light—even at dusk, when wildlife activity is greatest.

TOP PHOTO SHOWS BIRD AS SEEN WITH THE NAKED EYE. BOTTOM PHOTO SHOWS BIRD SEEN WITH 7X BINOCULAR.

LITTLE BLUE HERON AT DUSK

For wildlife watching in the close quarters of woodland streams, in swamps, or around small ponds, always locate wildlife first with your naked eyes. Then use your binocular to zero in for closer observation.

In wide-open spaces such as a large wetland expanse, along a shoreline, the surface of a big lake, and the ocean, use your binocular to slowly scan the view and search for wildlife. You may spot a white gull on a sparkling wave, a green heron on a leafy mangrove, or a snake draped on a snakelike vine. Look carefully at every distinctive shape and form. I know this from experience. In Vermont, what looks like a stump in the water could be a moose, shoulder deep, feeding on water lilies. And more than once, what I thought was a dark clump of waterside brush turned out to be a bear drinking.

FEATHERED COMPANIONS

I watched the fisherman's boat move slowly
down the narrow canal, returning from the sea.
It had been a good day. I could see that the hole
was packed with ice and fish—grouper,
yellowtail, and dorado. High up on the boat's
flybridge, the captain steered a straight and
steady course down the narrow Florida Keys
waterway between boats docked to his port and
starboard sides. On the afterdeck, the sunburned
mate sharpened his knife, preparing for the job
of cleaning the catch. And accompanying the
boat, flapping all around the stern, were hungry
pelicans. The smell of fish was in the air, and a
feast was in the offing.

A white heron sailed down from a sea grape
branch, alighted on the boat's bow, and rode on
to the dock. On the dock a snowy egret waited,
squawking excitedly as the boat approached.

Soon the mate was cutting and filleting fish,
throwing unwanted parts into the water, where
the pelicans fought greedily over every scrap.
The mate discarded the largest bones and
fins—pieces that could choke even a pelican—
in a waste can that he kept beneath the
cleaning table.

On the edges of the table stood the heron
and egret, waiting patiently, watching every slice
of the mate's sharp knife. As he worked, the mate
spoke softly to them. Then he cut some thin
strips of bloodred flesh from one dorado's tail and
threw each bird a helping.

On the water, birds are your constant
companions. Even when you think you're all alone
wading in a forest stream or drifting offshore in a
boat, there are birds to keep you company. They
sing from waterside trees. They flit from branch to
branch. They swoop out over the water to snatch
insects from the air. Once, while I was

standing in a pond and changing fishing flies, a cedar waxwing flew from shore and perched on the very tip of my fly rod. I held the rod straight and still until the colorful bird flew away.

On big, freshwater lakes and out on the ocean, fishermen rely on the presence of gulls and cormorants to find large schools of fish. Birds swooping and diving always mean that there are fish below the waves. And later when the boats return to port and people clean their catch, there are always birds to take the scraps.

A SQUADRON OF PELICANS WAITS FOR FISH SCRAPS.

OFFSHORE BIRDS

Offshore, inshore, on salt water and fresh water, birds spice up every outing. They call and squawk. They flap and glide. They float and wade. They animate the scenery—water, trees, and sky.

OSPREYS AND EAGLES

GULLS AND TERNS

STORKS AND CRANES

PELICANS

CORMORANTS AND ANHINGA

DUCKS AND GEESE

HERONS AND EGRETS

IBISES

SANDPIPERS

SPOONBILLS

Deanna and I always
carry a camera to
photograph the
beautiful birds we
see on the water.

THIRSTY PILGRIMS

One warm, overcast April afternoon, in anticipation of the opening day of trout season, I visited my favorite beaver pond. As I stepped out of the woods into the broad clearing created by generations of beavers felling trees, I spied a large, dark shape out in the shallow water. Through my binocular, I saw that it was a black bear standing in the water up to its haunches. The bear was drinking water and feeding on marsh grass. It was completely unaware of me.

Gauging from the size of the beaver lodge, which was also in my binocular field of view, and allowing for the part of the bear that was underwater, I estimated the animal to be four feet high at the shoulder. Its weight I guessed was close to four hundred pounds. The bear was coal black, except for its muzzle, which was dark brown. As

it munched a mouthful of wet grass, the bear's bottom jaw rotated much the way a cow's jaw moves when chewing. I focused sharply on the bear's broad black nose and whiskered snout. Then I focused on the bear's shining black eyes. At first they were looking away. Suddenly they were staring directly at me! The bear stopped chewing.

I stood very still, with the binocular pressed against my eyes. Without taking its eyes off me, the bear raised its muzzle and sniffed the air.

A few minutes into the standoff, I felt my knees buckle. Almost involuntarily I sank into a crouch. My arms were tiring from holding the binocular up to my eyes. My hands began to tremble very slightly, and the image of the bear shook in the lenses. Finally the bear turned and ran splashing in the shallow water. When it reached the far side of the clearing, it stopped, turned around, stood tall on its hind legs, and looked across the divide to see if I was still there. I was. The bear plopped down on all fours and shuffled off into the forest.

To a fisherman wading or a canoeist quietly paddling along, a sudden encounter with a large animal such as a bear or a moose can be unnerving. But I have learned that as long as you keep at least fifty feet of water between you and the wildlife, you will be safe. The animals are only thirsty, or they have come to eat aquatic plants, and they are not aggressive. This is not the case, however, on salmon rivers with bears competing for the fish.

Salmon fishermen know to stay far away from fishing bears.

More commonly seen quenching their thirst at the water's edge are deer, foxes, coyotes, and raccoons. At dusk I look for raccoons on the shore, digging in mud for crayfish. Raccoons like their food wet, so once they catch a crayfish, they stay, dipping and soaking the crayfish in the water between crunchy bites.

At night the shyest and most secretive animals leave the cover of shoreline cattails, brush, or woods and make their daily pilgrimage to the water. Paddling quietly back to shore after

A PAIR OF RACCOONS
IN A MANGROVE SWAMP

an evening on the water, you might get a glimpse of one of these animals. But most often you will know they have come only by the tracks they leave in the wet soil. Here, a mouse scurried out, wet its whiskers, and scurried right back. There, an opossum came to drink. And look at those bobcat footprints showing how slowly and sneakily and reluctantly the animal came out in the open to quench its thirst.

GATOR TRACKS IN MUD

SEMIAQUATIC ANIMALS AND TRUE AQUATIC ANIMALS

I was fishing for barracuda off a rocky Florida shore. The tide was going out. The water was very shallow and extremely clear. There was a lot to see. Some crabs were underwater, crawling in the crevices between the rocks. Some were out of the water, scurrying over the wet shoreline boulders. Dozens of spiny black sea urchins were clinging to the rocks. Most of them were submerged, but a few had spines poking out of the water. In the gentle current, a sea

CORMORANT ON A ROCKY SHORE

SEA URCHINS ON A ROCK

cucumber rolled and bumped against a chunk of brown coral, upon which a barnacle-encrusted stone crab stood like a tiny samurai, challenging everything that drifted near.

Under the coral, small black-and-yellow-striped sergeant fish hovered in the undulating flow. A school of mullet swarmed by, their dorsal fins and tails breaking through the water surface. Following the mullet, a thousand tiny emerald shiners swam as one. I cast my shiny spoon lure and reeled it through the crowd. The shiners made way for the flashing lure without a single fish breaking ranks.

I was about to cast again when, out in the channel, a seabird suddenly emerged with a fish in its beak. The cormorant gulped the fish down, and then, lowering its head underwater, began swimming toward shore. The bird looked to the right and left underwater as it kicked itself along with wide webbed feet, coming closer and closer until it was literally swimming at my feet!

CORMORANT WITH FISH IN BILL, AS SEEN FROM DIRECTLY ABOVE

I watched up close as the bird snorkeled over the urchins, over the sergeant fish and shiners, obviously hunting for something it had not yet seen. The cormorant dived completely under, keeping its body angled downward as it probed between the coral and rocks with its long, pointed beak. It was the first time I had ever actually seen a cormorant as it hunted for food underwater. With its legs spread and its webbed feet waving and its black feathers all slick and wet, it looked more like a fish than a bird. It finally found what it was searching for, snapped the tiniest of crabs in its beak, and swam to the surface to crunch it up.

Animals that spend much but not all of their time in water are considered semiaquatic. Cormorants, anhingas, loons, and grebes are semiaquatic birds. Muskrats, beavers, otters, and mink are water animals as much as they are land animals. All amphibians are semiaquatic. And so

are certain species of lizards, turtles, and snakes.
Alligators and crocodiles are reptiles that hunt
and cool themselves in water, but they nest and
rest and sun themselves on land. There are even
some semiaquatic crabs that dig burrows in shore
land, and others that climb waterside trees.

Semiaquatic animals
are many and varied.

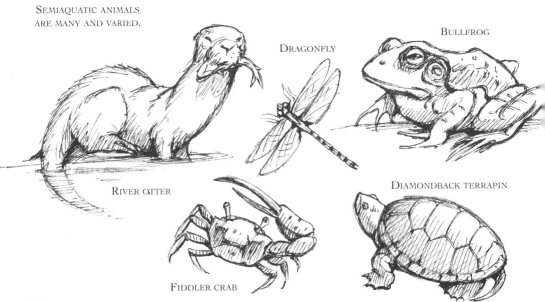

Dragonfly

Bullfrog

River otter

Fiddler crab

Diamondback terrapin

Fish, dolphins, whales, and manatees live their entire lives in water. They are true aquatic animals. I have seen a dolphin leave the water and chase a school of fish right up onto the beach. But the dolphin quickly wriggled back into the surf. Dolphins are agile enough to do such things. Whales are not. When a whale mysteriously becomes beached, it takes an army of rescue workers to get the heavy animal back in the water.

MANATEES, DOLPHINS, WHALES, AND FISH ARE AQUATIC ANIMALS.

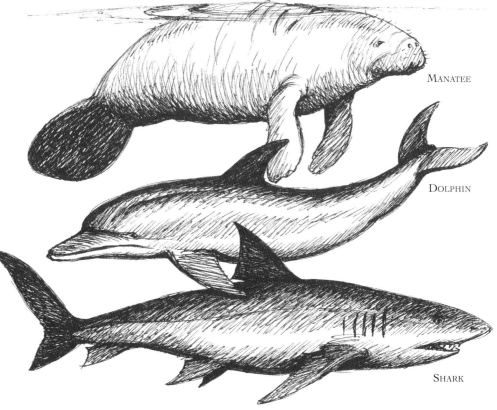

MANATEE

DOLPHIN

SHARK

FINS AND TAILS

A shark's triangular dorsal fin cuts a long straight line through the water before lowering under and out of sight. Sometimes both the dorsal and tail fins stick out of the water. This was the case when I watched that huge hammerhead attacking the tarpon. You may recall that I saw the big shark's dorsal fin and five feet behind it was the shark's tall tail fin. The size and shape of both fins were clues to the shark's identity.

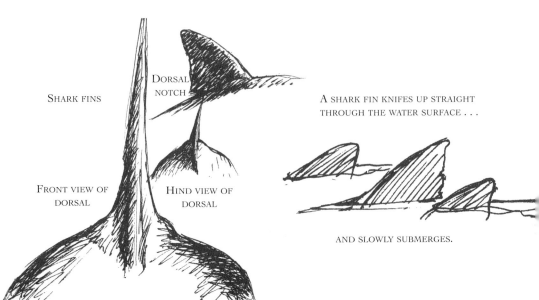

SHARK FINS

DORSAL NOTCH

FRONT VIEW OF DORSAL

HIND VIEW OF DORSAL

A SHARK FIN KNIFES UP STRAIGHT THROUGH THE WATER SURFACE . . .

AND SLOWLY SUBMERGES.

No notch

Shiny back

A dolphin's dorsal fin is also triangular, and its size in proportion to the animal's body is similar to that of a shark. But a dolphin's dorsal fin pops up out of the water and goes down, up, and down, in the vertically undulating fashion of all swimming mammals. Since a dolphin's tail is horizontal like a whale's tail or a manatee's tail, it never knifes out of the water behind the dorsal fin the way a shark's tail does.

Dolphin tail

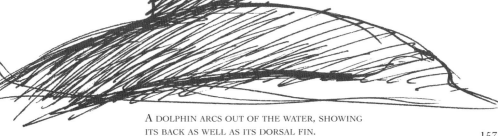

A dolphin arcs out of the water, showing its back as well as its dorsal fin.

Distinguishing sharks from dolphins by their fins and the way they move in the water takes a sharp eye and some knowledge of the animals. I've made a study of identifying fish by their fins and tails. In my journals there are many pages of sketches and notes devoted entirely to this unique and fascinating form of wildlife watching.

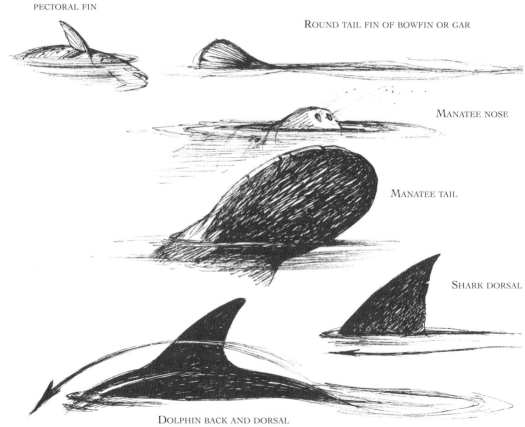

TROUT TAIL

TROUT PECTORAL FIN

ROUND TAIL FIN OF BOWFIN OR GAR

MANATEE NOSE

MANATEE TAIL

SHARK DORSAL

DOLPHIN BACK AND DORSAL

JACK CREVALLE DORSAL AND TAIL

PERMIT DORSAL

STINGRAY "WINGS"

BARRACUDA TAIL AND DORSAL

BONEFISH TAIL FIN WEAVING
BACK AND FORTH

BONEFISH TAIL

BONEFISH DORSAL AND TAIL

REDFISH TAIL

TARPON DORSAL

SAILFISH DORSAL

MARLIN DORSAL

KILLER WHALE DORSAL

159

WATCHING AND WATCHING OUT!

Every year a number of manatees need to be rescued, but not because they have become beached or are stranded on shore. They are rescued because they are sick or injured. Manatees are very sensitive to temperature changes, and a sudden cold spell can be lethal. They are also vulnerable to red tide—a naturally recurring population explosion of toxic bacteria in the water. And there are manatees that have been injured and seriously wounded by the sharp blades of boat propellers.

PROPELLER SCARS
ON BACK

The Florida manatee lives only in the shallow waters of Florida's rivers, lagoons, and bays. They are also found swimming in the boating channels and coastal flats around the Florida Keys. An adult manatee can be twelve feet long and four feet wide, and weigh one thousand pounds or more. They are as slow moving as they are huge and simply cannot dodge the spinning blades of a boat propeller churning by. So many manatees bear cuts and scars from collisions with boats that biologists studying manatees can identify many individual manatees by the shape and pattern of the propeller marks in the animal's skin.

Motorboaters in Florida must go slowly when cruising in shallow water and keep a lookout for manatees. Manatee areas are posted with signs warning boaters to slow down. Deanna and I have seen manatees surfacing to breathe in saltwater channels that were busy with boat traffic. We have seen manatees in seaside marinas hanging around the docks where dripping hoses provide fresh water to quench a manatee's thirst.

And once, in Florida Bay, we saw a manatee actually scratching its back on the hull of a boat. It happened to be the boat we were on!

We were preparing for a long sail out to Butternut Key. I wanted to see the baby sharks reported to be there. Our vessel was a thirty-foot-long sailing sloop named *Windsong*. The captain's name was Tom. Captain Tom decided it would be best to motor out of the busy marina and set sail once we reached the open water of the bay. He pull-started the small outboard motor, which was clamped to the boat's transom, and let the engine idle while we uncovered the sails. As the little motor warmed up, a small stream of water squirted from the water-cooled shaft. I noticed a manatee moving toward the boat. It lifted its head out of the water and opened its mouth to drink the outboard's cooling water. But this was not fresh water from a hose.

It was salt water and not very good for a manatee to drink. Our captain quickly stopped the engine and the stream of water, hoping the manatee would

swim away. Instead, the manatee rolled over and began scratching its side on the boat's hull.

We waited and watched. The manatee would not go away. Deanna and I noticed that there were no propeller scars at all on the manatee's body. This manatee was not fully grown, and it had a lot to learn about the dangers of boats and propellers. After a long while, the manatee stopped scratching and slowly swam away. We cast off for Butternut Key, wondering how long the manatee's luck would last with all the boat traffic in the marina.

We didn't see any baby sharks at Butternut Key. The water was too murky. But on our sail we saw large stingrays and whole pods of dolphins leaping and skipping over the water surface. Some dolphins raced close alongside of the boat. The sight of dolphins is always cheery and joyous, but the nearness of the dolphins racing our boat was nothing short of magic.

A wild dolphin may look friendly. It may even follow and play in the water around your boat. But if you hold bait out for the dolphin to take in its mouth, you are playing with danger. A dolphin has sharp teeth, and it could accidentally bite your hand as it snatches the bait. Dolphins in marine parks and aquariums are tame and trained to be gentle. Wild dolphins are not trained. They do not behave or perform the way we'd like them to. They are free to do what they want.

Any wild animal being fed by hand may bite the hand that feeds it. Every time you reach toward or touch a wild animal, it will behave unnaturally or erratically and could become dangerous. Stay a comfortable distance away and you can watch most animals to your heart's content. If they are potentially dangerous animals, be sure to keep them in sight. The ones you lose sight of or those you are unaware of are the ones that can hurt you.

Some of the Most Dangerous Water Animals

Rattlesnakes (all species)

Cottonmouth moccasin

Brown watersnake (nonvenomous but bites aggressively)

Soft-shell and snapping turtles (Both can inflict severe bites.)

Crocodile

Alligator

Stingrays (all species)

Sharks (all species)

Barracuda

Moray eel

Man-o'-war jellyfish

Fire coral

Long-spined sea urchins

In alligator country, we do not ever walk along the water's edge, even if there are no tall grasses or plants growing onshore. An alligator can swim entirely submerged and it can stalk in water with only its eyes above the surface. When we do see an alligator, we stay at least fifteen feet away. No matter how small, an alligator is a dangerous animal. If we see a large alligator or crocodile in the water or on a grassy bank, we stay twenty-five feet away. A big alligator can move surprisingly fast when it attacks.

Baby alligators are the most dangerous alligators to approach too closely. They always have a very protective mama hidden close by watching over them. Deanna and I once came upon a group of baby alligators in the Everglades. We stepped back and scanned the area, looking for their mother. She was nowhere to be seen. Using a powerful telephoto lens, I began videotaping the little alligators swimming around in the amber-

LOOK CLOSELY AT THIS DRIED PALMETTO AND YOU'LL SEE A WATERSNAKE COILED INSIDE.

colored pool. As I stared through the viewfinder and focused sharply on the active little alligators, I noticed something submerged in the water beneath the floating babies. It was the two open eyes of their mother staring back at me.

In streams or lakes or swampland where trees stick up out of the water, snakes draped precariously on overhanging branches can accidentally fall. When canoeing in such wooded waterways, keep an eye out overhead for snakes, and take care not to bump or ram your boat into any tree trunks. You could end up with a very frightened and defensive snake as a passenger. In southern swamps and bayous, palmettos should be regarded with caution.

A small snake can climb a palmetto and coil within the heart of the palm frond. I've seen small brown water snakes do this, as well as small cottonmouth moccasins. Either snake will bite. The cottonmouth bite can kill.

COTTONMOUTH
MOCCASIN
CROSSING A
FLORIDA TRAIL

Deanna and I never walk a narrow bank between water and tall plants. This is what I call Snake-bite Alley. Water snakes, cottonmouth moccasins, and rattlers coil at the edge of grasses or cattails to sun themselves and to ambush small animals that come to drink. Just stepping too close to a coiled snake can provoke a strike.

In northern Vermont we have very few water snakes, venomous or nonvenomous, and no alligators. But we do have great, big snapping turtles. Snapping turtles are usually not aggressive toward people. One may strike if you happen to step right on it. Most of the time, however, these big turtles sense you coming and move away before you get too close. Nevertheless, I watch for them in the water I wade in, and on overgrown stream banks where a depression in the vegetation could turn out to be a huge snapping turtle napping in the sun.

In salt water, danger can be nestled in the sand, swimming just beneath the surface, or floating in the waves. Stingrays often bury themselves up to their eyes in the sandy ocean floor and remain motion-less, watching for prey. When I wade where stingrays are commonly seen or caught by fishermen, I shuffle my feet in the soft bottom as I walk. This warns any buried stingrays of my approach, and they scoot away. Shuffling your feet as you wade is also an excellent way to avoid getting your toes pinched by a belligerent crab.

More and more people are wearing wading shoes in the water. Wading shoes help protect your feet from crab claws, broken shells, and sharp-edged coral. They won't protect your ankles or legs from the stings of jellyfish swimming by, so watch

STINGRAY
HIDING UNDER
SANDY BOTTOM

MAN-O'-WAR

out for these gelatinous drifters, and when you see one, step aside to let it pass. Not all jellyfish sting, but until you learn which ones do and which ones don't, do not touch any and do not let any touch you. Jellyfish sting to immobilize small sea animals that they capture and eat. The sting is caused by tiny, poisonous barbs in a jellyfish's food-trapping tentacles.

MOON JELLYFISH AND THE UPSIDE-DOWN JELLYFISH CAN CAUSE MINOR STINGING.

The tentacles of a man-o'-war jellyfish are long and far-reaching, and a man-o'-war sting is considered the most painful sting in the sea. As beautiful as they are dangerous, man-o'-war jelly-fish resemble festive blue and purple balloons. When you see one floating on the waves or washed up on the beach, give it a wide berth.

MAN-O'-WAR
WASHED ONTO
BEACH

The tentacles can be spread out and around, or
broken off and lying separately on the sand.

Shark! The word alone can cause fear and panic.
In fact, when I'm fishing and I see a small shark that
I want to point out so Deanna can also enjoy seeing
it, I am careful not to say "Shark" too loudly. I might
frighten other people on the beach.

No matter what you've seen on TV or in movies,
sharks will not rocket onto the beach and pull
you off your blanket. As long as you are on the
beach and not in the water you are in no danger of
being bitten by a shark. If you are in the water and
the water is clear and you are not splashing around
to obscure the clarity, sharks that happen to be near
will see you and most likely will swim away. Even
the notorious bull sharks and dreaded
hammerhead sharks that prowl the edges
of shallow water appear to have little interest
in people. They are looking for fish to eat.
And unless you resemble a big snook or a
tarpon, you are not on their menu.

THE NURSE SHARK IS NONAGGRESSIVE,
YET IT ACCOUNTS FOR MANY SHARK BITES—
MOSTLY FROM SNORKELERS GRABBING THEM.

Why is it, then, that every year a number of people are attacked by sharks? It could be that certain sharks that have been hand-fed by people have come to associate humans with food. The sport of swimming with sharks and feeding them by hand may be having a negative effect on the way sharks view human beings. A shark taking a piece of fish from a diver's waving hand might one day mistakenly take a hand from a swimmer's waving arm.

Marine biologists believe that most shark attacks on humans are cases of mistaken identity. Many victims of shark attacks were swimming in murky water, or in the surf where shells and sand are churned up by waves. Or they were swimming after sundown, when visibility underwater is low. If a shark cannot see its prey, it may naturally move toward any movement in the water. The actions of a swimmer kicking in the water duplicate the movement of a wounded fish or even a seal.

A SHARK'S DORSAL FIN DOESN'T ALWAYS SURFACE.

Fishermen standing rock steady in the surf, or wading slowly in clear, shallow water, are in very little danger of being mistaken for food. I have had a few close encounters with sharks, but when the animals saw me standing in the water, they quickly swam away. And when these shark encounters occurred, I was not off on some lonely and exotic island that only adventurers go to. I was in the same water as swimmers and shell collectors.

Every person who swims or wades in the ocean is in shark habitat. Seeing a shark heightens our awareness of their presence. Most of the time, however, sharks swim unseen, and we are blissfully unaware of them. But don't worry: You can enjoy the ocean and be perfectly safe, as long as you use common sense. Don't go in the water with an oozing cut or if you are bleeding in even the slightest way. Before you swim, remove bright and shiny jewelry. A silver bracelet or anklet flashes in the water much the way a small fish flashes. Stay out of murky water, and never swim in the ocean after dark. Surf fishers who

CHUM IS A MIX OF FISH
BITS FINE ENOUGH TO
FILTER THROUGH A
MESH BAG TO ATTRACT
BIG FISH.

fish near swimmers should not use chum.

It could attract sharks as well as the fish it is intended for.

Finally, where an unusual number of shark attacks are being reported, stay out of the water. Something is drawing sharks to the locale, and until the attraction fades, the water is not safe. When it comes to sharks, always choose prudence over bravery.

One morning in the Florida Keys, after a very stormy night, I went fishing on some nearby flats. The tide was low, and the water was quite clear, considering the recent wind and rain. I waded in up to my knees about fifty feet from shore and cast my lure another hundred feet out onto the waves. Suddenly I found myself engulfed by a large, swirling patch of dirty water, a remnant from the storm. I could no longer see my feet, let alone the ocean floor. To make matters worse, dorsal fins of lemon sharks appeared less than fifty yards from where I stood. The gray triangular fins cut long lines through the water surface. I was tempted to run to shore. Instead, I waded very slowly out of the dirty water into clear water, where I knew the sharks would see me standing tall and looking very human. Then, as the gang of sharks moved closer and closer, I slowly and quietly retreated to the safety of the shore.

The sun was going down over the mangrove islands. My son-in-law Chuck and I had been out on the ocean all afternoon trying something new. We were sight-fishing for bonefish. Our guide Rich stood high on the boat's stern-mounted platform, poling us silently over the shallow flats. We were all watching the sea grass beds for subtle signs of bonefish — small puffs of coral dust where a bonefish was rooting on the bottom for a crab, or the slender shadow of a bonefish on a white sandy shoal. Bonefish are almost invisible because their silver sides reflect the green color of the water.

Earlier, in the bright midday sun, I had my initiation to this special kind of fishing when Rich suddenly pointed over the bow of the boat and announced, "Fish at twelve o'clock!" Chuck and I looked in the direction but saw nothing but sea grass. "Now they're at one o'clock! Look!" Rich pointed impatiently over the right of the boat's bow. I adjusted my gaze. There they were! A shadowy group of three or four. According to plan, I was to be the first to cast. I stepped up on the bow and waited anxiously as Rich poled the boat closer and closer to the fish. "Wait . . . wait . . . wait . . . " he said. Then he gave the okay. "Cast! They're moving to the left! Cast to the left of the fish!"

Clumsily, I lobbed my line and live shrimp bait in the direction of the fish. The shrimp plunked into the water and sank. "Wait . . . wait . . . " Rich said. All three of us crouched low. The boat drifted toward the fish, and the fish worked their way on the bottom toward the bait. Suddenly my line tightened, and a hooked bonefish was racing away over the flats. I could barely hold on to the rod. I reeled when I could. Mostly I held on with both hands as the fish stripped hundreds of feet of ten-pound test line

off the spool. The reel's drag
sizzled. The line streaked
through the water. It was
overwhelming! My arms
shook under the strain.
This bonefish was the
strongest fish I had ever
hooked.

After four powerful
runs, the fish finally
gave in and I reeled
it to the boat.

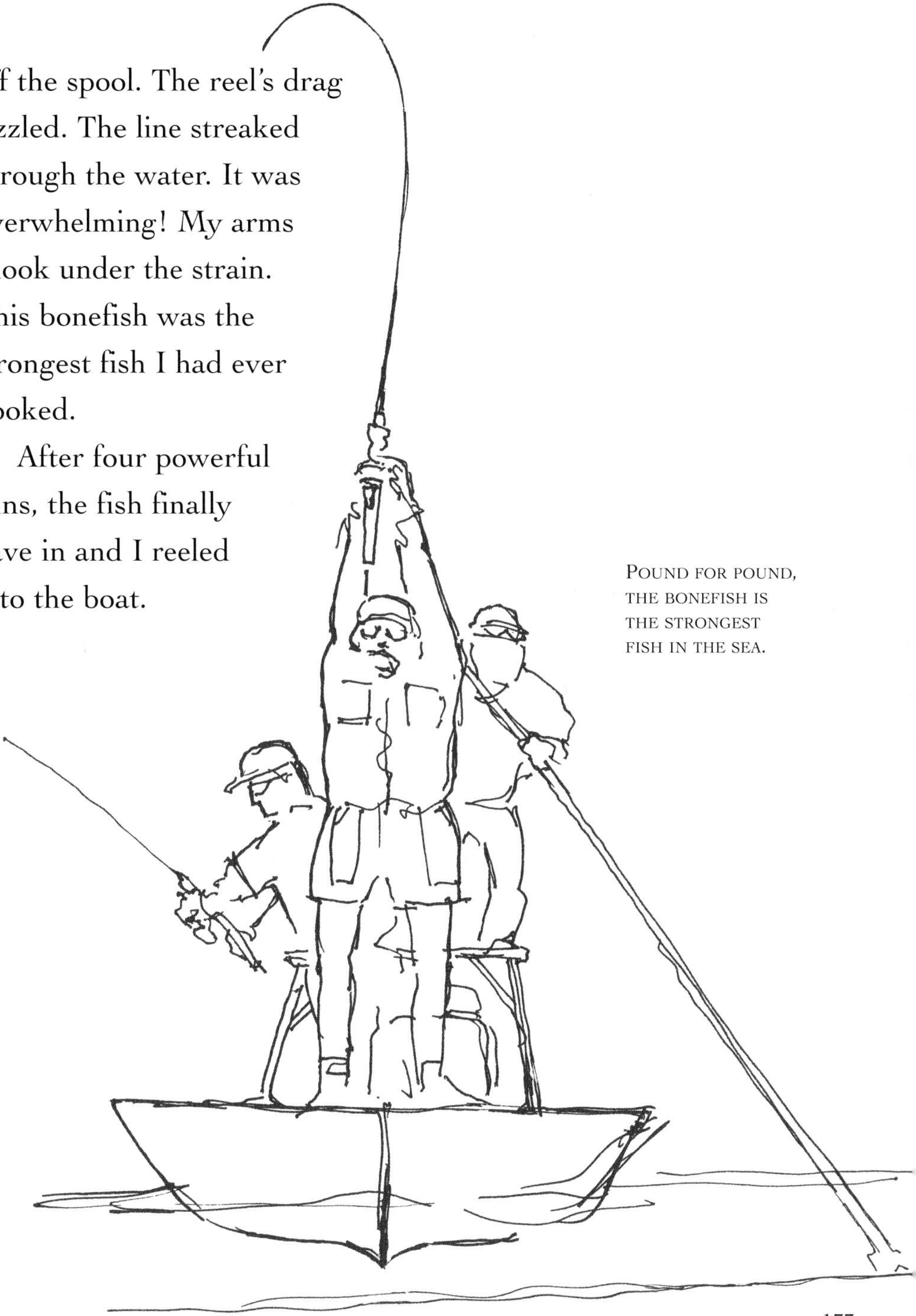

POUND FOR POUND,
THE BONEFISH IS
THE STRONGEST
FISH IN THE SEA.

It weighed only six pounds—big for a bonefish, but small compared to its power and strength. Chuck snapped a picture. It was my first of two bonefish for the day. Chuck caught the biggest fish—a nine-pound bonefish that made his arm so sore, the pain bothered him for the rest of the day.

My guide, Rich, and me

Now it was sundown, and the water rapidly darkened until we could no longer see to search for puffs of bottom dust or shadows of bonefish on the sand. Now we were watching the surface of the water for bonefish tails poking out of the rippling waves. The tide had receded. There was less than a foot of water under the boat. Long rays of orange sunlight outlined the edges of the boat's bow. Out in the dark water, in the angled sunlight, we saw tails!

BONEFISH "TAILING" AS THEY FEED IN VERY SHALLOW WATER

A whole squadron of bonefish were tailing toward us, each tail glowing orange in the sun. It looked like a flotilla of tiny sailboats tacking this way and that way through the water. We did not speak. We barely moved. The tails came closer. It was mesmerizing. I forgot I was fishing. And when Rich told me to cast, I was not prepared. Hastily, I hurled my bait right onto the fish and spooked the whole school.

The sun was down. The day was done. Rich poled the boat off the shallow flats to deeper water and then started the 115-horsepower Yamaha. With a flick of a finger, he switched on his night-running lights and took off full throttle toward the marina. Chuck and I held on to our hats. We couldn't believe our luck. Between us we had caught and released three trophy-sized bonefish! But it was the sight of the fish tailing in silence—no line being reeled, no words being spoken, just the sunset and the watching—that we brought back with us.

SCENES FROM JUST ONE DAY OF A LIFETIME OF FISHING, BOATING, AND WATCHING WATER WILDLIFE

Some Sample Fishing Journal Pages

THE BONEFISH EXPERIENCE GAVE ME TWO
FANTASTIC PAGES IN MY JOURNAL.
KEEP A FISHING JOURNAL AND
TRY TO RECORD ALL YOU
REMEMBER ABOUT YOUR
DAYS OUT ON THE WATER.

longer upper lip than lower jaw

brilliant turquoise blue when aggit.

blue spots too

olive green bars

all silver scales

bonefish 7 lbs
caught by Jim Armstg
off Bud & Marys Marina
on a live shrimp.
Caught off Teatable key

right green fins

back color whitebelly fades to silver

Top of mouth longer than lower lips & jaw

olive green back + bars

perfect 3/4 profile

perfect top of head shape

acute back

this is low conspicuous

This suggests the scales perfectly!

white mouth
Silvery cheeks w/ pink edge

more like this

fan light green w/ blackish edge

belly + underside Pure white + scaled like rest

crushers inside mouth top + sides.

hard outside ridge

tongue

you have to lift the rod up and hold it above your head when the fish takes off. Or else it will create slack + break away.

Chuck caught a 9/6. bonefish
and hooked two others, one near

rays / bonefish / crushers / sharks / bonefish tail color

We fished for them at high noon - 1 - 3:30 PM by looking for the puffs of their digs and then spotting their shapes swimming.

Puffs from diggings in the coral dust for crabs + shrimp.

Dorsals + tail   tail   Dorsal

At sundown and low tide we fished for them by seeing their tails + dorsals sticking out of the water.

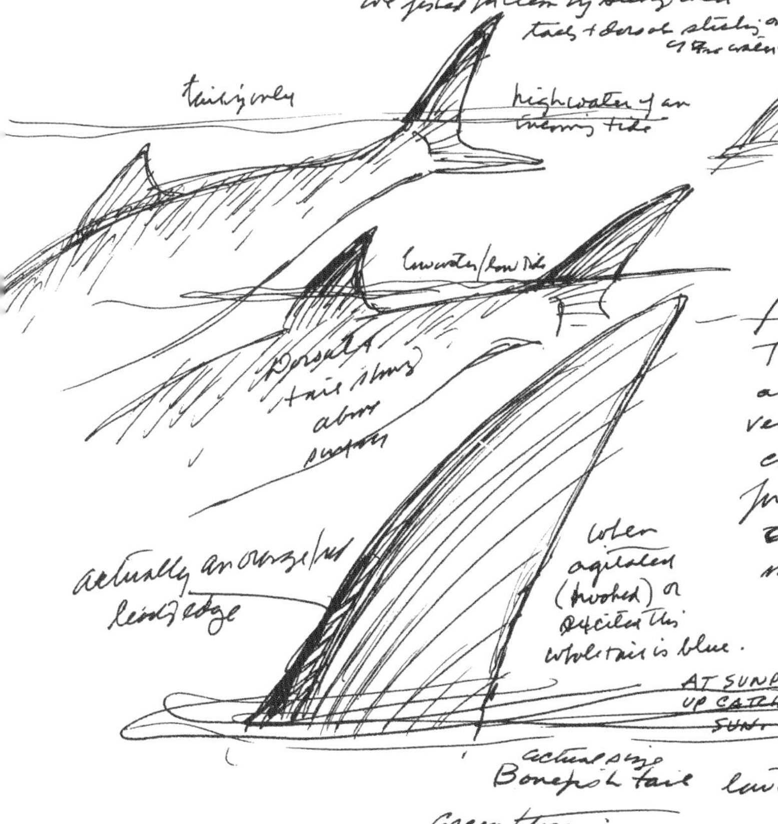

tailing only   high water of an incoming tide

Low water / low tide

Dorsals tail shown above surface

actually an orange/red leading edge

color agitated (hooked) or excited this whole tail is blue.

The tail zigs + zags this way that way as the fish feeds

You point until the guide gets you pointing in the right direction to see.

This only occurs at low tide or in very shallow water and could only last for an hour or so before the tide that is returning makes the water too deep to show the tail.

AT SUNDOWN THESE TAILS LIGHT UP CATCHING THE LOW ANGLE OF THE SUN. IT IS QUITE BEAUTIFUL TO SEE THEM KNIFING THROUGH THE WAVES.

actual size Bonefish tail   low tide / sundown

Green/turquoise

white underwing

saw three eagle rays today

— We fished tailers so closely to the boat the guide said it was the closest he'd ever gotten to the wary species. This fish was only 6 or 7 feet away - tail up out of the water.

Here's another journal page. This one is about mullet.

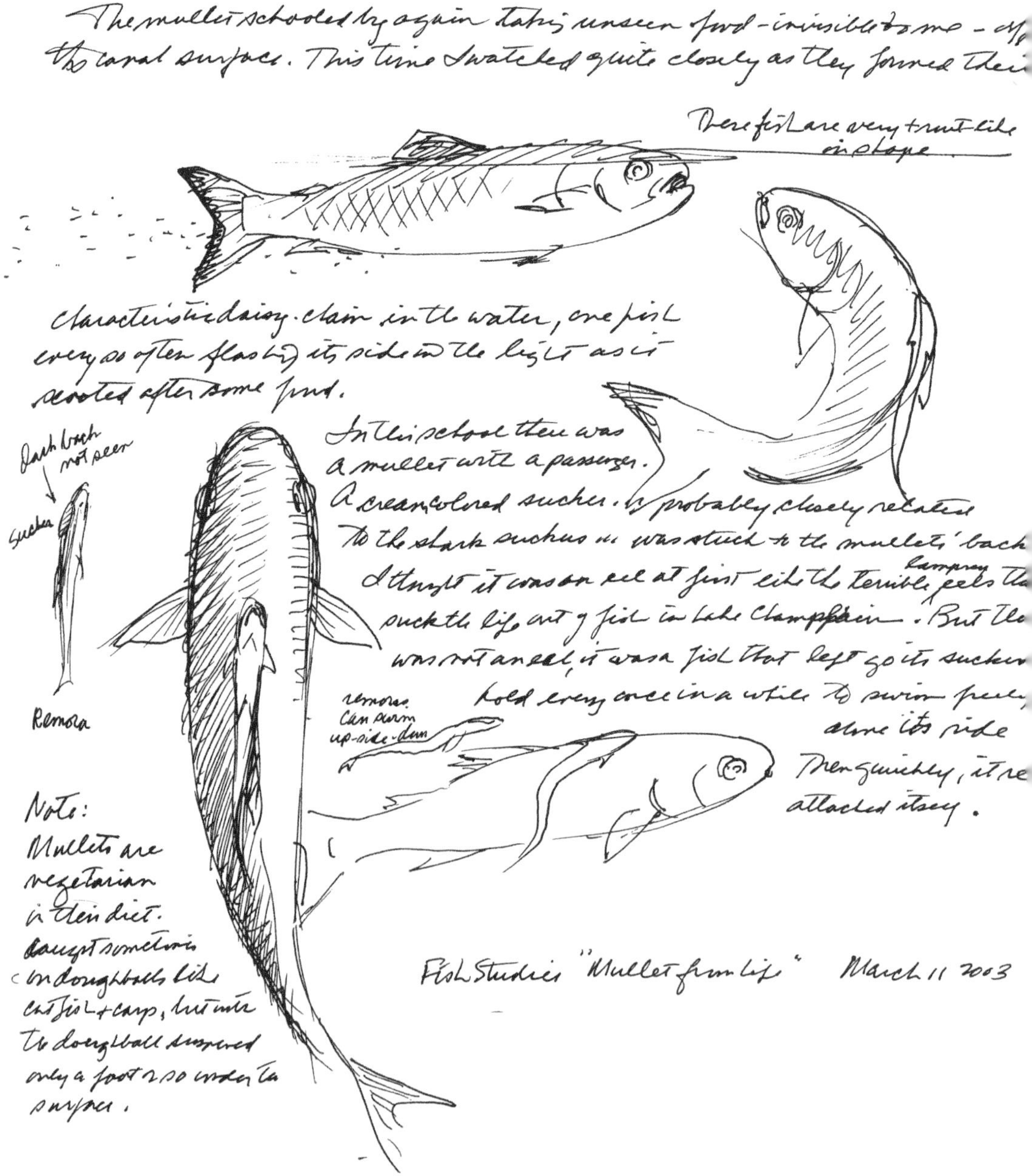
The mullet schooled by again taking unseen food - invisible to me - off
the canal surface. This time I watched quite closely as they formed their
These fish are very trout-like in shape.
characteristic daisy-chain in the water, one fish every so often flashing its side in the light as it scooted after some food.
Dark back not seen
sucker
Remora
In this school there was a mullet with a passenger. A cream colored sucker. is probably closely related to the shark suckers. It was stuck to the mullet's back. I thought it was an eel at first like the terrible lamprey eels that suck the life out of fish in Lake Champlain. But this was not an eel, it was a fish that let go its suckers hold every once in a while to swim freely alone its side.
Then quickly, it re attached itself.
remoras can swim up-side-down
Note: Mullets are vegetarian in their diet. caught sometimes on doughballs like catfish + carp, but note the doughball suspended only a foot or so under the surface.
Fish Studies "Mullet from life" March 11 2003

Appendix

Some North American Freshwater Fish Species by Region

NORTHEAST REGION
Brook trout
Yellow perch
White perch
Crappie
Largemouth bass
Sunfish
Bullhead catfish
Muskellunge
Pickerel
Northern pike
Landlocked salmon
Sturgeon
Bowfin
Walleye
Rainbow trout
Brown trout
Sucker
Lake trout
Carp
Eel
Longnosed gar

Channel catfish
Freshwater drum
Blue catfish
Rock bass
Stonecat

SOUTHEAST REGION
Largemouth bass
Smallmouth bass
Rainbow trout
Brook trout
Eel
Longnosed gar
Alligator gar
Sunfish
Crappie
Bullhead catfish
Channel catfish
Blue catfish
Flathead catfish

MIDWEST REGION
Blue catfish
Channel catfish
Lake trout
Largemouth bass
Landlocked salmon
Sucker
Muskellunge
Walleye

Northern pike
Yellow perch
Rainbow trout
Sunfish
Smallmouth bass
Pickerel
Brook trout
Brown trout

SOUTHWEST REGION

Rainbow trout
Golden trout
Black bass (smallmouth bass)
Brook trout

NORTHWEST REGION

Sturgeon
Grayling
Steelhead trout
Kamloops trout
Cutthroat trout
Dolly Varden trout
Coho salmon
Pacific salmon
Sockeye salmon
Rainbow trout
Lock leven trout
Brook trout
Brown trout

Some North American Saltwater Fish Species by Region

EAST COAST

Atlantic salmon
Giant bluefin tuna
Swordfish
Bluefish
Yellowfin tuna
Marlin
Channel bass
Shark
Amberjack
King mackerel
Tinker mackerel
Spanish mackerel
Sailfish
Marlin
Bonefish
Barracuda
Needlefish
Houndfish
Ladyfish
Triggerfish
Tarpon

Wahoo
Dolphin (dorado)
Yellowtail snapper
Grouper
Red snapper
Redfish (channel bass)
Halibut
Flounder
Fluke
Sea trout
Cobia
Flying fish

GULF COAST
Tarpon
Red snapper
Sea trout
Sawfish
Dolphin (dorado)
Sailfish
Marlin
Amberjack
Sea bass
Wahoo
Leatherjack
Barracuda
Ladyfish
Needlefish
Shark

WEST COAST
Typee salmon
King salmon
Chinook salmon
Striped bass
Pacific salmon
Steelhead trout
Flying fish
Broadbill swordfish
Dolphin (dorado)
Tuna
Marlin
Yellowtail snapper
Wahoo
Shark
Sailfish
Albacore
Sea bass
Halibut

Index

When I was a boy, I dreamed of adventure.